PRAISE FOR *HAVING AND BEING HAD*

"Biss's new book, *Having and Being Had*, enlivens her own critique of capital in the 2020s by delving into the trouble we all avoid discussing—and then staying with it. Using quiet anecdotes about her neighbors, family, and friends and references ranging from *Scooby-Doo* and *The Americans* to Emily Dickinson and the Dire Straits video for 'Money for Nothing,' street photographer Vivian Maier and IKEA, Biss examines capitalism in the Trump era through our fixations and anxieties." —*Los Angeles Times*

"A sensational book . . . Keenly aware of her privilege as a white, well-educated woman who has benefited from a wide network of family and friends, Biss has written a book that is, in effect, the opposite of capitalism in its willingness to acknowledge that everything she's accomplished rests on the labor of others."

—Associated Press

"Incisive, impressive, and often poetic . . . [Biss] turns what is essentially a chronicle of white guilt and anxious privilege into a thoughtful and nuanced meditation on the compromises inherent in having a comfortable life." —*The Wall Street Journal*

"Sharp and snappy. . . . *Having and Being Had* picks apart the ethics behind our capitalist society, culminating in a powerful look at the ways in which we assign value to the people, places, and things that comprise our lives." —*Time*

"A major achievement. . . . With astute consideration, this expansive and intimate accumulation asks the questions that touch all our lives." —Claudia Rankine, author of *Citizen*

"Biss has long been drawn to topics that lend themselves to polemic, which she approaches in a spirit that's resolutely unpolemical. Her intellect is omnivorous, roving, and humane." —*The Cut*

"Biss has an eye for subtle points of style, an ear for double entendres, and a taste for teasing the irony out of both. . . . She is a consummate poet of discomfort, well able to navigate the awkwardness of saying things usually left unspoken."

—Irina Dumitrescu, *The New York Review of Books*

"If you feel weird about your privilege and role in capitalism, then much of this incisive essay collection will resonate with you. If not, you should read it anyway—perhaps especially then."

—*Good Housekeeping*

"Through Biss's inquiry, one is reminded that capitalism is not inevitable and that currency goes well beyond the money in one's pocket. This collection is curious, sharp, funny (truly), and full of questions we, as a society, have forgotten how to ask about how we spend, what we buy, why we work, what labor is, and how we calculate worth."

—NPR's *All Things Considered*

"The accumulation of these pieces disassembles and reassembles a class the way it is built—through time: by turning over its assumptions, policy, and language in the hand. This is an essential book for our out-of-control times of greed."

—John Freeman, *Literary Hub*

"A brilliant, lacerating reexamination of our relationship to what we own and why, and who in turn might own us in ways we didn't know we consented to—what could be more necessary now?"

—Alexander Chee, author of *How to Write an Autobiographical Novel*

"[Biss writes with] confidence, accessibility, and provocation . . . [Her] writing is calm and precise, without flourish, so clear it belies the difficulty of writing prose so crystalline." —*Chicago Tribune*

"Excellent . . . Biss is unflinching when broaching [her] often taboo subjects, and approaches them through a personal lens, writing about her own experience with homeownership, gentrification, marital equality, motherhood, and being a working artist."

—*Refinery29*

"A collection of essays circling elegantly around the object of her study. . . . [that is,] the moments we realize that consumerism has begun to rust our souls." —*The New Republic*

"Delicious . . . Biss is not only unafraid of taboo, she leans into it. She uses the form of the essay to interrogate, break apart, and complicate something in order to make it fully known and understood. . . . Disarming and effective."
—*The Washington Independent Review of Books*

"In this witty, genre-bending book, Eula Biss smashes the taboo against talking about money with exhilarating results. Her investigation ranges from the strictly financial to the broadly philosophical as she accounts for her life with disarming honesty and grace." —Jenny Offill, author of *Weather*

"With her signature moving and relatable prose, Eula Biss wrestles honestly with the everyday contradictions that accompany the effort to be a good person (and a good artist) in a capitalist world."
—*ARTnews*

"Compulsively readable . . . A book that asks to be read, absorbed, and read again." —*BookPage*

"Eula Biss is known for stepping off the plank into turbulent waters that others might fear or avoid, armed with wry wit and a radical lucidity. *Having and Being Had* continues this journey, offering us a probing tour of capitalism and class that sidesteps posturing and jargon in favor of clarity, humility, and incitement."
—Maggie Nelson, author of *The Argonauts*

"No contemporary writer I know explores and confronts her own societal responsibilities better than Eula Biss."
—Aleksandar Hemon, author of *The Lazarus Project*

HAVING

AND BEING HAD

Eula Biss

RIVERHEAD BOOKS
NEW YORK

RIVERHEAD BOOKS
An imprint of Penguin Random House LLC
penguinrandomhouse.com

Copyright © 2020 by Eula Biss
Penguin supports copyright. Copyright fuels creativity, encourages diverse
voices, promotes free speech, and creates a vibrant culture. Thank you for
buying an authorized edition of this book and for complying with copyright
laws by not reproducing, scanning, or distributing any part of it in any
form without permission. You are supporting writers and allowing
Penguin to continue to publish books for every reader.

Riverhead and the R colophon are registered trademarks
of Penguin Random House LLC.

Grateful acknowledgment is made for permission to reprint the following:

Excerpts from "Two Tramps in Mud Time" by Robert Frost from
the book *The Poetry of Robert Frost* edited by Edward Connery Lathem.
Copyright © 1969 by Henry Holt and Company. Copyright © 1936 by
Robert Frost, Copyright © 1964 by Lesley Frost Ballantine. Reprinted
by permission of Henry Holt and Company. All rights reserved.

"Free Flight" by June Jordan, from *Directed by Desire: The Collected Poems
of June Jordan*, edited by Sara Miles and Jan Heller Levi, Copper Canyon
Press, 2005. © 2005, 2020 June M. Jordan Literary Estate Trust.
Used by permission. www.junejordan.com.

Excerpts from *Peyton Place: A Haiku Soap Opera* by David
Trinidad, Turtle Point Press, 2013. Copyright © David Trinidad.
Reprinted by permission of the author.

The Library of Congress has catalogued the
Riverhead hardcover edition as follows:

Names: Biss, Eula, author.
Title: Having and being had / Eula Biss.
Description: New York : Riverhead Books, [2020] |
Includes bibliographical references.
Identifiers: LCCN 2020010815 (print) | LCCN 2020010816 (ebook) |
ISBN 9780525537458 (hardcover) | ISBN 9780525537472 (ebook)
Subjects: LCSH: Leisure—Social aspects. |
Work—Social aspects. | Quality of life.
Classification: LCC HD4904.6 .B57 2020 (print) |
LCC HD4904.6 (ebook) | DDC 306.3—dc23
LC record available at https://lccn.loc.gov/2020010815
LC ebook record available at https://lccn.loc.gov/2020010816

First Riverhead hardcover edition: September 2020
First Riverhead trade paperback edition: August 2021
Riverhead trade paperback ISBN: 9780525537465

Printed in the United States of America
5th Printing

Book design by Meighan Cavanaugh

for John

in love and debt

I am afraid to own a Body –
I am afraid to own a Soul –
Profound – precarious Property –
Possession, not optional –

—EMILY DICKINSON

If we really want to understand
the moral grounds of economic life
and, by extension, human life,
it seems to me that we must start instead
with the very small things.

—DAVID GRAEBER

CONSUMPTION

ISN'T IT GOOD?

We're on our way home from a furniture store, again. What does it say about capitalism, John asks, that we have money and want to spend it but we can't find anything worth buying? We almost bought something called a credenza, but then John opened the drawers and discovered that it wasn't made to last.

I think there are limits, I say, to what mass production can produce.

We just bought a house but we don't have furniture yet. We've been eating on our back stoop for three months. Last week a Mexican woman with four children rang our doorbell and asked if our front room was for rent. I'm sorry, I said awkwardly, we live here. She was confused. But, she said, it's empty.

It is empty. I hang curtains to hide the emptiness, but it remains empty. There wasn't any furniture in the house where

I grew up until a German cabinetmaker moved in with us. He arrived in a truck so heavy that it made a dent in the driveway. He filled our dining room with his furniture and then he made tiny replicas of that furniture with the machines he brought in the truck. I still have the tiny corner cabinet with lattice doors, the tiny hutch with brass knobs, and the tiny dining room table with expertly turned legs. They're in the basement, wrapped in newspaper. The tiny dresser sits atop my dresser, which is from IKEA.

The apartment we just left was furnished with shelves that John made out of cheap pine. They're in the basement now, reduced to lumber. The ammunition box that I found on the curb and made into a coffee table is in the backyard, planted full of marigolds. I hate furniture, my father once murmured. He had just visited a warehouse full of furniture made of unfinished pine. This was after the cabinetmaker went to a nursing home and his furniture went away too. As a child, I burned a hole in the dining room table. The cabinetmaker, who smoked a pipe, supplied me with matches. I loved to burn things, but I felt remorse over the table, which I also loved.

The lyric *I burned a hole in the dining room table* is tethered, in my mind, to the liner notes of a Billie Holiday album that I borrowed from the library in college. She was singing songs written by someone else, the notes explained, but she rewrote them with the way she sang. Her delivery transformed a banal portrait of moneyed life into a wry critique of that moneyed life.

In the furniture stores we visit, I'm filled with a strange unspecific desire. I want everything and nothing. The soft colors of the rugs, the warm wood grains, the brass and glass of the lamps all seem to suggest that the stores are filled with beautiful things, but when I look at any one thing I don't find it beautiful. "The desire to consume is a kind of lust," Lewis Hyde writes. "But consumer goods merely bait this lust, they do not satisfy it. The consumer of commodities is invited to a meal without passion, a consumption that leads to neither satiation nor fire."

In the end, all the furniture we buy will feel like lyrics written for someone else's song, except the dining room table made by the Amish. This table will be solid cherry, a beautiful wood. It will be well made, but not quite as well made as the table I grew up with, the table I burned. To get a table like that, we would need to spend much more money. Or we would need a German cabinetmaker to move in with us.

I once had a girl / Or I should say, she once had me, the car radio sings. John and I both fall silent. It's been a long time since I've heard this song. And I don't know if I've ever really listened to the ending. What happened there, I wonder. Did he make a fire in the fireplace while the girl was at work? No, John tells me, he burned her place down. He is sure of this, but I am not so sure.

I can't stop thinking about it. Norwegian wood. It bothers me. Soon I'm reading interviews with the Beatles. "It was pine really, cheap pine," McCartney said about the wood paneling that inspired the title. About the ending, he said, "It could have meant I lit a fire to keep myself warm, and wasn't the décor of her house wonderful? But it didn't, it meant I burned the fucking place down."

SLUMMING

I return to my old apartment building to get the bike lock I left in the basement. What are you doing here, my downstairs neighbor asks, slumming? She never liked me. She worked until 2:00 a.m. and always went to sleep around the time my toddler woke up in the morning. In revenge for the sound of his feet she vacuumed at night. She owned a house before she moved to this building, but she got out of that game she said and now she owns a bar.

Slumming was a pastime for women of the owning class in Victorian England. They visited the poor, wrote reports, and put girls to work doing laundry, boiling and scrubbing and iron-ing the linens of the rich to make the girls clean, redeemed by work, while the women read them poetry. The women imag-ined themselves in service to the poor, but the poor served them. A woman went slumming, Alison Light writes, to find herself "beyond the narrow confines of her well-upholstered world." Slumming sometimes became a profession for women who had no other access to work. They ran homes where orphans and poor girls were raised to be good servants. Among those girls was the foundling Lottie Hope, who grew up to become Virginia Woolf's maid.

The second of the two bedrooms in our apartment was intended to be the maid's room. This building was once a lakeside retreat, a vacation home far from downtown Chicago. But the tenants now are not on vacation. When we moved in, kids with cigarette burns were crawling in and out of their mother's apartment through the broken screen of a window in the building next door, and a man who had lost his mind was screaming from his window onto the alley. Our windows faced the lake, which made me feel rich. Bums fished for steelhead on the rocks by the lake and waves sent huge plumes of spray over the pier. Dogs ranged over the sand, their leavings drying in the sun. An old woman who sometimes yelled at me sat on a bench facing the lake. I live farther from all this now. And farther from the lake, with its postindustrial water reflecting the storm clouds blowing in from the horizon.

That's it? my landlord asks when he sees me. I used to talk with him nearly every day on my way out of the building. And for years, I rode a bike that he gave me, a bike that a former tenant left behind.

I linger in the concrete courtyard, talking with the hairdresser who used to cut my hair in her kitchen. Above the hairdresser lives a chef who used to bring me bags of arugula when it was in season, and above her is a sculptor who used to drink wine with me. The widow of a postal worker lives above the apartment that was ours. In one of our few exchanges, she told me that she loved Toni Morrison and I gave her my signed copy of *Sula*. Across the courtyard are a rug salesman, an actor, and a woman who wrote the screenplay for a movie I've never seen. There is also a girl who owns a flock of lacy underwear that roosts on the clothesline in the basement. I'm suddenly feeling the loss of all this. The man with a drinking problem who gave my son a see-through frog lives here, and the man with a meth problem who gave him an Easter basket full of plastic cockroaches. My son won't remember those men, but the cockroaches will continue to crawl though my life, even in the new house.

COMMERCIAL

Our house is a brick bungalow, nearly identical to the house next door. These houses were built by brothers, both dead now. I learn this from my neighbor, who lives in the other brother's house. He's a retired postal worker and a saxophone player who still practices every day, though his health is too poor now for him to perform. The interiors of our houses are the same, he tells me, except for my attic, which the former owners of our house renovated. He would like to renovate his attic, too, but he doesn't have the money. Some relatives of his are in prison and all his extra money goes to supporting their families. I guess God, he says, doesn't want me to have money. I'm not sure, but I think he's joking about God.

He has told me, already, about attending the same elementary school my son attends, and of being beaten on the playground. He has told me that he couldn't, in those days, risk a conversation with a woman like me. He had to keep his head down when he passed a white woman on the sidewalk, he said, and just respond, Yes, ma'am, if she spoke to him. He has told me, also, of refusing a holiday turkey offered to him by the owner of a mansion by the lake, a rich man who demanded that he wade through deep snow to deliver packages to the service entrance at the back of the house.

The former owners of our house, who were white, made extra money by allowing the house to be used as a set for commercials. John discovers this when he gets a call from a casting agent who wants to know if the house is available. It's not available—we live here. But then we learn how much we will be paid. All we have to do is leave the house for three days and two nights and we will earn $8,000.

The commercial is going to be for Walmart, the corporation that produced the fortunes of four of the twenty richest people in this country. Walmart couldn't build stores in Chicago for years but they're here now, despite ongoing protests over low wages, and they want their commercial set in a classic Chicago bungalow. We don't own anything from Walmart but this doesn't matter because Walmart furniture is moved into the house, Walmart curtains are put up, and some Walmart prints are hung on the walls in Walmart frames. A white set designer and a white director work to create an authentic African American interior. The commercial, they tell us, is going to feature an African American grandmother serving a holiday turkey.

Next door, in the house just like ours, lives an actual African American grandmother, the wife of the retired postal worker. We're getting paid to have our house made over to look like what a set designer imagines their house looks like so that Walmart can try to sell things to people who look like them. John tells all this to his friend Dan, who says, I think that's the definition of white privilege.

UNDERSTANDING

I don't understand, my mother says. How is that the definition of white privilege? This isn't the first punch line she's
ruined.

My mother dropped out of high school and later, after college
and a divorce, she nearly dropped out of the middle class. She
still has white privilege, but she often does not have hot water.
I admire how thoroughly she has discarded the life she was
born into, the silver in the sideboard and the opera on the
record player. She has kept only the books.

In one of the fairy tales she told me as a child, a girl is pursued
by a witch. As the girl runs, she throws behind her the things
she carries in her pockets, the things her mother has given
her. She throws down a hairbrush that becomes a thick forest. She throws down a hand mirror that becomes a lake between her and the witch. You must throw away everything
you've been given, my mother might say. That much I understand. But it has only just occurred to me to wonder what

witch she's running from. And if her witch will be my witch, too.

She used to trade eggs from her chickens to a neighbor for expired bread, still good. And when she drove us home from school she would stop at a dumpster behind a restaurant to salvage fruit, also still good. I once asked my mother if she had a retirement account and she laughed at me. I've never had anything like that, she said. And then she said, after a pause, My children are my retirement account. You were my investment.

She had four children by the time she was thirty but she had no income, no contributions to social security. I was still childless at thirty and already working for the university. I have a retirement account, which puts me in a poor position to explain privilege to my mother. Nobody understands privilege as well as those who don't have it. I guess, I tell her, I don't understand either.

THE RIGHT WHITE

I'm taking possession of the house by painting it, every room. And the question of what color in what room is consuming me. I think maybe I should start with historical colors, but I can see the original color of the walls under the layers of chipped paint: cloying pink. Maybe memory, not history, is the place to start. Buttered Yam, from my mother's garden. Evening Blue, an old bottle half-buried in the dirt. Forest Moss, the color of my mother's little living room, which smelled like woodsmoke.

Color(ed) Theory Suite, a work in which artist Amanda Williams painted houses slated for demolition on the South Side of Chicago, began as a collection of colors: Harold's Chicken Shack Red, Crown Royal Purple, Pink Oil, Ultrasheen Blue, Flamin' Hot Orange, Currency Exchange Yellow. "This palette combined my Ivy League academic training as an architect with my lived sensibility as a South Side native," she says. Each house was painted a single color, from the bricks of the foundation to the shingles on the roof. She painted only houses that weren't worth anything to anyone. Not to dealers, not to squatters, not to neighborhood teenagers. *Zero-value* was her term. And she painted these zero-value properties in colors drawn from products sold to black people. Every color, she says, is a code.

I'm having trouble finding the right white. I don't like Opulence White or Chantilly Lace or French Manicure. This conversation is boring, my sister complains. Maybe I'll give up on white, I tell her, and paint the living room peach. Peach is problematic, she says, laughing at me now.

I've discovered a brand of paint that I can't afford. But I could buy it. To afford something like paint, for someone of my class, is to announce your values, most often, not your financial capacity. I can't admit to valuing paint that costs $110 per gallon. But I find this paint unbearably luminous, and undeniably better than any other paint. At night, when my family is asleep, I study paint swatches from the hardware store and then I open the heavy folds of the catalog from Farrow & Ball and run my fingers over the small squares of paint, slightly raised in estate emulsion. Even the names are better: Matchstick, String, Cord, Skimming Stone. These are not aspirational whites—these whites can afford to be modest. One is even called Blackened.

I remember the great revelation of moving up from acrylic paints in high school to oil paints in college. First just black and white on paper and then a full set on canvas. They were worth the expense, those silken oils in their slim metal tubes. I loved all the colors, especially the cadmium orange, which was slightly toxic. Flamin' hot. This is the closest I've come to painting in years, shopping for paint.

I send a swatch of Sulking Room Pink to Robyn, knowing she'll appreciate the name. "To sulk" in French is *bouder*, the source of *boudoir*, a woman's private room. A room of one's own, in a dusty, moneyed pink. And then there's Etiquette, a white described as "a well-mannered hue." It's a white that's hiding behind its own whiteness. Another line for this white poem. My mind is on paint now more often than poetry. I've found a new literature: Crisp Linen, Collector's Item, White Zinfandel, Pashmina, Fine China, Ivory Tower, Mirage White, American White.

Benjamin Moore has declared Simply White the Color of the Year. This, in the year a white man will be elected to the White House. The selection of white as the Color of the Year was "inevitable," the creative director of Benjamin Moore explains. "The color white is transcendent, powerful, and polarizing—it is either taken for granted or obsessed over."

I obsess, which solves nothing. Deep in Thought is my favorite name for a white, but I don't really like the color. I wouldn't want my walls Deep in Thought. On my way to a parent-teacher conference I stop in the hallway of the elementary school to photograph a huge box of institutional toilet paper, the color listed on the label as Empathy White. Maybe that's the color I'm looking for. Or a variant, a concerned off-white like All Apologies. Or something more revealing, like Paperwork White or Payroll White. Or maybe I should just paint it all Property.

NOT CONSUMERS

The catalogs keep coming. I don't know how they find us, or how to make them stop. Sometimes two of the same catalog arrive on the same day. They accumulate in piles, outdoing each other with heavier paper and richer colors. Then the Restoration Hardware catalog arrives, like a parody of the whole problem, in two volumes, each the size of a telephone book. They are bigger and heavier than my grandfather's two-volume set of *Illustrated English Social History*. We put the Restoration Hardware catalogs near the fireplace and sit on them.

The IKEA catalog has a message on the front: "Designed for people, not consumers." In the photograph, some young people are having a fun, unfussy dinner at a crowded table. There are dirty dishes piled on a cart and a guitar is leaning against the wall. The IKEA catalog sits on top of a pile of catalogs with photographs of sterile rooms showcasing furniture that has never been touched. This other, messier way of life, IKEA suggests, is not just less expensive, it is more human.

John and I have a set of two dressers from IKEA and Nick and Robyn have the same two dressers. Nick's is his second of this dresser—the bottoms dropped out of all the drawers in the first one. It was like a building with a perfect facade, Robyn said, where all the floors had collapsed into the basement. I remember a brownstone in New York City like that, with trees growing inside. And a foreclosure in the suburbs still pristine on the outside, but stripped of all its fixtures inside, even the wires and the pipes.

The dresser is simple and Shaker in its design. Shakers believed that the end of the world was near, which would seem to be an argument for temporary furniture, but making something built to last was, for them, an act of prayer. "Do all your work as if you had a thousand years to live," Mother Ann Lee told her brethren, "and as you would if you knew you must die tomorrow."

There aren't many Shakers left. Their furniture has outlasted them, as it was meant to. Their values, I was told by a tour guide at the village where Ann Lee died, were embodied in their furniture. I wonder if a Shaker dresser, taken out of the context of Shaker life, still embodies the Shaker dedication to celibacy and hard work. Perhaps it whispers to its owner at night. Maybe my dresser is where my doubts come from.

At the village where Ann Lee died, which I visited as a school-child, I saw Shaker chairs hung on pegs and I was taught to sing a Shaker song. The furniture didn't interest me, but I was captivated by the song, especially the last two lines: *To turn, turn, will be our delight / Till by turning, turning, we come round right.*

In my twenties I moved ten times. On the fourth or fifth move, when I was leaving New York, I left behind a bed frame that my mother had made. It was simple and spare with no headboard, Shaker almost, and designed for celibacy in that it was narrower than a single bed. My mother was upset when she learned that I had abandoned it. I tried to explain that I wasn't leading a life that allowed for furniture.

In California, I slept on a slab of foam that could easily be rolled up and moved anywhere. My boyfriend, who kept his clothes in a large cardboard box, suggested that we make all our furniture out of cardboard boxes. It was an idea that had already been pioneered by IKEA, who made particleboard end tables with hollow interiors. "The ease of self-invention that IKEA enables is liberating," Lauren Collins writes, "but it can be sad to be able to make a life, or dispose of it, so cheaply." Within a year, I had rolled up my mattress and moved my boxes to Iowa, where I found my furniture on the street.

"A better everyday life for more of the many," is IKEA's mission, on paper. I think of all the IKEA furniture that I have seen eaten by life. The end tables with broken legs, the cracked slats of futon frames, the particleboard desks left out on the curb and destroyed by the rain before they can be taken to a new home. IKEA, the third largest consumer of wood in the world, has made furniture into something that gets used up. It is furniture for the apocalypse. But what I like, what makes me laugh a little about "for people, not consumers," is the implication that consumers are not people.

LIVING THINGS

Things are like people, Maggie tells me, alive in theory. Maybe people are just so much like things, I think, that we recognize ourselves in flickering light bulbs and empty bottles. I'm reading *My Life with Things: The Consumer Diaries* by Elizabeth Chin. She writes, "People are so completely and so powerfully alienated that they are reduced to things; in the meantime, the things they produce and the things they purchase have acquired all the livingness that people have lost."

Her book is a diary of lost livingness. In one entry, she has just suffered a miscarriage, and she walks through Target bleeding, allowing herself to buy two chairs she's been wanting. The next day, still bleeding, she goes to IKEA and buys a small table for the chairs. She imagines a Mastercard commercial: "Chairs, $79 each; clock $23; table $39. Getting through a miscarriage: Priceless."

She's an anthropologist, and these diary entries are field notes on her life. She is studying herself the way she once studied poor black children. A professor, she has an annual household income over $90,000, which puts her in the top 20 percent of earners in the richest country in the world, ever in human history. She knows that she belongs to an economic elite, but she doesn't feel rich. She feels stretched thin by the work of paying her bills and cleaning her house. She doesn't want to pay a woman to clean her house, that's too intimate, but she pays a woman to wax her legs in the pink privacy of a nail salon's back room. She lives a life of contradictions and she's caught between her own contradictory desires. She wants more and less at the same time, just as I do.

"What I really want, really really want, is to work less," she writes. But she also wants an antique rug. She loves a particular rug owned by her godparents, who cared for her when her mother couldn't. When she visits her godparents and sees the rug, she can't think about anything else. She wants them to offer the rug to her, but they don't. They have already given her a rug. She wants this rug so badly that she feels "ripped off." It's as if her godparents have stolen something from her by having a rug that she wants. Her desire has made it hers, and her desire has imbued it with the livingness she's losing as she begins to hate her godparents for having the rug. She feels disgusted with herself. But still, she wants the rug. "One of the main things Marx noticed about capitalism," she writes, "is that it really encourages people to have relationships with things instead of with other people."

I'm tired from work, but I take the train downtown to meet Mara at the Kemang Wa Lehulere exhibit. I watch Mara move around the gallery, examining each work and making notes in her notebook. I've only taken a few steps and have not quite committed to looking at anything. On the wall next to me is a giant chalk drawing of a pencil sharpener, the kind that used to be attached to the wall over the wastebasket in elementary school classrooms, with a pile of bones underneath. Beyond that is a series of broken ceramic dogs next to open suitcases full of living sod. This art demands some interpretive work. I move around the gallery without really focusing my eyes, hoping not to be found out. I feel like I'm failing the art, too tired to work. Finally, I pretend to watch a video playing on a loop until Mara suggests that we get some dinner.

On our way out of the museum we stop in the gift shop, where I find the ability to focus my eyes. I've been wanting a necklace, I remember, and there are glass cases here full of necklaces. I gravitate to one that's made from bronze castings of the tiny leaves of a plant. This necklace was once alive. It costs $200, twice as much as my wedding ring. But I go ahead and buy it. This gives me a strange sense of accomplishment that persists through dinner. On the train home I'm still too tired to read, but I feel like I've done something today. Or the necklace has done it for me.

CONSUMERS

"A metaphor is all this really is," David Graeber writes. He means *consumption*, which was once the name for a wasting disease, and is now the word anthropologists use for almost everything we do outside of work—eating, shopping, reading, listening to music. *Consume*, he notes, is from the Latin *consumere*, meaning "to seize or take over completely." A person might consume food or be consumed by rage. In its earliest usage, *consumption* always implied destruction.

Consumption was the opposite of *production* in Adam Smith's *Inquiry into the Nature and Causes of the Wealth of Nations*. He made this inquiry in 1776, when work was being relocated into factories and lives were newly divided between home and work. We still use the math of that time to subtract what is consumed at home from what is produced at work. In that crude equation, only work that earns money is productive. And as long as there's no third quantity, like reproduction, the equation works out to zero.

She ate it, my father told my sister years ago, when she wondered what happened to my stereo. This was during my first year in New York and the money for the stereo was a gift from my father, who had told me that he would pay for my college tuition and nothing else, ever. He had three more children to send to college. The stereo was an exception, a surprise for my birthday, and I did eat it. I wanted a stereo but I needed food.

Food is destroyed by our consumption but silverware is not, though the metaphor behind the word suggests that we eat up even our own silverware and dishes too. "We should think about how far we want to extend the metaphor," Graeber warns. Yes, we consume fossil fuels, in the "eat up, devour, waste, spend" sense of the word. But we don't consume music. Music becomes part of us, as food does, but it isn't destroyed in the process.

What is destroyed when we think of ourselves as consumers, Graeber suggests, is the possibility that we might be doing something productive outside of work.

HUSBANDRY

There's wallpaper under the old paint in the living room and it's buckling slightly. I show John a corner that I found curling up behind the radiator. He grips the corner and pulls, tearing a huge sheet of wallpaper off the wall, exposing plaster beneath. I feel like we're going to get in trouble for this. But the house is ours. John begins to strip the rest of the room. He works with a lamp on the floor, which projects my shadow onto the newly naked wall. Stay there, John says, and he uses a carpenter's pencil from his toolbox to trace the outline of my shadow directly onto the plaster. Touched, I trace his shadow next to mine.

We're still there under the new paint, two shadows joined in pencil. We were married without paperwork, on our own authority. And then we were married again years later, for health insurance, in a courthouse with forms and fees. Marriage, my mortgage, a document not intended to be understood. At the signing I tried to read every page until I realized how many pages there were, and then I just committed my name, again and again. Not to ownership, but to the promise of payment.

The house isn't mine. I don't own it so much as I take care of it. This occurs to me as I work on the roses, cutting away the old canes. I don't like the roses, but I care for them because they came with the house. As I prune them, I have the sense that all of this—the brick the roses climb, the lath and plaster, the copper pipes, the oak floors, the coal room, the cracked slab on which it all rests—is a gift. Not to me, but to the future. The house is just passing through my hands. It's not a purchase, it's a husbandry.

I'm in service to the house. The truth of this is married to the other truth, that the house serves me. I can borrow against this asset, which will grow in value if all goes well. But a house, my grandfather warned me just before we bought this house, is a place to live. Not an investment.

THE NEIGHBORHOOD

The growl of a muffler wakes me at midnight and I turn to John in the dark and say IROC. You can expect it to come back around the block in twenty minutes, John says. He knows the habits of the IROC.

Before we bought this house, John asked the real estate agent what the neighborhood was like. He paused before he answered—he was forbidden by law from describing demographics. He couldn't tell us, for instance, that most of the black people on this block have lived here a long time and that most of the white people have recently moved in. He told us, instead, that he had just sold the house two doors down to a family who planned to rehab it, and that the house across the street is a recent rehab too. There's a dealer on the corner, he said. On the other corner there's a man who stays home with his children while his wife teaches. And the man who lives over there, he pointed, works on his cars in the street.

The leaves weren't on the trees yet when we moved in, so we could see over our next-door neighbor's lawn and across the street through the open doors of the garage around the corner. There was a car with its hood up and a car on a jack in the garage. And there was a car with a thrumming muffler revving up in the driveway. That's an IROC, John said, with reverence. And then he said, I want a relationship with that guy.

The man with the IROC plays Sade and Genesis and Chaka Khan and Human League out of his garage while he works on his cars. His music is our summer soundtrack, along with the marching band practicing at the high school two blocks away and the saxophone playing jazz standards in the basement next door. Wherever we are, in the house or the yard, we look up and say IROC when we hear it. It's close enough to rattle the glass in our windows, but far away, in the sense that it's on the side of the street where no white people live. We know the timbre and the tuning of the IROC. And we know the name of its owner now—I learned it from another neighbor. But we don't have a relationship with him.

GET OFF MY LAWN

I'm looking through a chain-link fence into a hole where, just yesterday, there used to be a house. A new house is going to be built here, a house two inches under the maximum height and worth over a million dollars. Get off my lawn, a woman says to me as I look into the hole. I didn't see her until now. She's an older black woman, standing on the porch of the house next door. I'm not exactly on her lawn, but I know that's not the point. The point is that she wants me gone. I'm your neighbor, I say, as if that solves anything. Get off my lawn, she repeats.

This woman's grandfather built her house, I'll learn later. She owned it outright and could have left it to her children but the property taxes kept going up in her old age. Someone selling loans convinced her to remortgage the house to pay her taxes, another neighbor tells me. And that's how she lost it. The bank owns it now, it's in foreclosure, but she's ninety years old and they aren't going to evict her. They're waiting for her to die. In the meantime, there's a tarp on the roof and two broken windows upstairs.

The block she lives on, and mine, are just inside the area shaded red on a Home Owners' Loan Corporation map from 1940. The description of the red area, the lowest rated, reads, "It is somewhat better than the average negro district for this class of population. Here live the servants for many of the families all along the north shore." The low rating was meant to discourage investment by banks and insurance companies. This effectively translated race into property value.

One block away from the hole in the ground, on my block, there's a small house on a lot that's narrower than the other lots. John met one of the women who live there when he ordered an Uber and she picked him up seconds later. She's a black woman who lives with her mother and she grew up in that house, which is about to go into foreclosure. It's a shame, this woman said to John, that so few of the old families still live in this neighborhood. And then she invited us to the friends-and-family weekend at her church.

THANKSGIVING

I'm upset about the gravy boat. And the roasting pan, and the coasters, and the platters, and the cheese plate. I don't want any of this. All I wanted was serving spoons for Thanksgiving dinner and John bought all these other things.

John laughs off my dark mood as he stuffs the turkey. I laughed at my grandmother, years ago, when the Thanksgiving dinner I was cooking in her kitchen upset her. See this, she said, showing me the thin ring of pumpkin I'd left in the bottom of a can. Waste! We have too much food, she moaned. All this food, and who's going to eat this banana before it goes bad? I'll have to, she said, stuffing the brown banana into her mouth angrily.

The gravy boat is ridiculous, John agrees. Nobody needs one. But we're hosting Thanksgiving for the first time in our own house and this occasion calls for a fucking gravy boat. It's absurd, I know, for me to spend this particular holiday feeling upset about having things I don't want. And I don't understand why I'm upset, other than that this all feels like too much. Even the phrase "our own house."

When we bought this house after years of looking, I was no longer convinced that I wanted a house. The money in our savings account was not money, in my mind, it was time. All those dollars were hours banked, to be spent on writing, not working. It seemed like a waste to spend time on property. I tried to bargain with John about the house. I wanted to know what he would trade me for my agreement to buy it. Nothing, John told me. Either I wanted the house or I didn't.

I wanted it. I wanted to paint the kitchen Moir Gold and I wanted to plant a garden in the backyard. I wanted to make something mine. What I wanted, more than anything, was the illusion of permanence the house provided. The solid foundation, the bricks that wouldn't blow away, the sense of security. That was a fantasy, I knew, but it felt real.

I light the wick on a candle shaped like a turkey, which will burn itself away, headfirst. "Killing wealth" is what the Haida people of the Pacific Northwest called their potlatch feasts. At these feasts, rank was established by how much a person could give away. Houses were burned at potlatches thrown by the Kwakwaka'wakw people, and sewing machines were thrown into the sea. But this was not typical of the tradition. This was the potlatch around 1900, after the Kwakwaka'wakw had been decimated by disease and were living in a new economy.

Unrecognized as citizens and unable to file land claims, they had lost most of their land to commercial fisheries and canneries. But they worked for wages in the canneries and could buy machine-made blankets and store-bought goods. They had more than they'd ever had before, in one sense, and less in every other.

Two artists can have all this? Nami asks when she arrives with Gus and Vu. She's marveling at the new dining table and the big empty living room. Not without paying for it, I tell her. Nami just quit her job and I'm jealous. I would gladly trade this gravy boat to quit my job, but I would also have to trade this house.

CAPITALISM

Bill and I are reading the same book and we've both marked the same passage: "Modernization was supposed to fill the world—both communist and capitalist—with jobs, and not just any jobs but 'standard employment' with stable wages and benefits. Such jobs are now quite rare; most people depend on much more irregular livelihoods. The irony of our times, then, is that everyone depends on capitalism but almost no one has what we used to call a 'regular job.'"

I never had a regular job until now. In my twenties I left job after job, working until I had enough money to write and then writing until I needed money again. I didn't know of any other way to live as an artist. Even the job I have now, my regular job, was temporary at first. I was an "artist in residence" and the contract required that I leave after four years. My residence was not permanent. But then the contract was revised, and revised again. When I could pass as permanent I bought a house.

Bill and I were temp workers, years ago, at the same publishing company in New York. Bill's task one day was to alphabetize hundreds of books on a huge set of shelves. He found many duplicates, like two copies of *The Grapes of Wrath* and three copies of *Market Wizards*. At the end of the day, after everyone had gone home, we put all the duplicates in a box and sold them at the Strand for $60. That much at least, we felt, the company owed us for the boredom of our work.

I worked for the editor of *Stock Market Wizards*, which was the sequel to *The New Market Wizards*, which was the sequel to *Market Wizards*. The purpose of this third book, the editor explained to me, was mainly to capitalize on the success of the first two books. *Stock Market Wizards* featured interviews with traders who made millions during "the glory days of the internet boom," and nearly all of them told stories about losing everything before they made it big. They lost houses, they lost life savings lent to them by relatives, and they lost marriages. They weren't wizards, just gamblers who could tolerate major losses.

The book Bill and I are reading now is *The Mushroom at the End of the World: On the Possibility of Life in Capitalist Ruins*. I've marked every passage about precarity. "What if, as I'm suggesting, precarity *is* the condition of our time—or, to put it another way, what if our time is ripe for sensing precarity?" And, "Precarity is the condition of being vulnerable to others."

I think of my time in New York, when I was so often lost. I was at the end of the line in Far Rockaway, looking for an address that didn't exist. I was walking sixty blocks down Madison Avenue, stopping at every store and restaurant to ask for a job. I was wandering the East River waterfront, past warehouse after warehouse, followed by a city bus that pulled over so the driver could tell me that I wasn't safe.

One of my first jobs in New York was visiting empty lots for the parks department. The city wanted to sell these lots, which had increased in value over the decades since they were abandoned. But the lots had been registered with the parks department as gardens. I took Polaroids through chain-link fences to make a record for the city that there were gardens there, and gardeners who would chain themselves to concrete blocks buried in the ground when the bulldozers came. The gardeners had cleared those lots of bricks and needles, and they had planted roses. They had invested in zero-value property. I walked from empty lot to empty lot and talked with every lunatic, every junkie, and every evangelist I met.

Maybe I need more precarity in my life, I tell Bill. Maybe I've become too comfortable. No, he reminds me, precarity has a price. And a person can be too vulnerable. After a pause, Bill admits that he doesn't really know what capitalism is. In trying to explain it, I realize that I don't know either. And I don't know where capitalism began, or when. We agree that we will find out what capitalism is before we talk again.

COMFORTER

The comforter is too big for our washing machine, but we no longer live within walking distance of a laundromat. I wonder what people who live in houses do when they need to wash their comforters? They drive in cars, I'm sure.

The closest laundromat has only one machine big enough for my comforter. I pack it into the washer and pour in the detergent and begin putting quarters into the slot. After two quarters, the machine is jammed. I find the attendant, who tells me this machine sometimes does this. It's broken. She shrugs. Out of principle, I ask for my two quarters to be returned. The retrieval of the quarters takes a long time.

As I wait, I think of all the time I spent in my twenties not having money. Not having money is time consuming. There are hours spent at laundromats, hours at bus stops, hours at free clinics, hours at thrift stores, hours on the phone with the bank or the credit card company or the phone company over some fee, some little charge, some mistake.

My comforter is sticky with detergent now. Carrying it across the street, trying not to get detergent on my clothes, I drop first the bottle of detergent and then the comforter. A car slows down for me. There's oil from the road on the comforter— the comforter is actually getting dirtier. And I won't be writing today. I feel like I'm going to cry. I drive to another laundromat, a huge one, with rows and rows of machines.

Now my comforter is spinning dreamily in clouds of bubbles, but I'm angry over how this day has gone. I didn't want to spend my time this way. I walk across the street to the Supreme Burrito. Sitting there, wearing my winter coat inside, eating a taco out of a plastic basket and waiting for a wash cycle to end, I have the sense that I'm reaching back and touching my former life.

My adult life, I decide, can be divided into two distinct parts—the time before I owned a washing machine and the time after. I consider the possibility that the washing machine, more than the house, has changed my life. I call my sister and tell her that what I've really done is buy a $400,000 container for a washing machine. As I say this, I'm aware that the cost of our house was closer to $500,000. But I don't say that out loud, it makes me too uncomfortable.

AFFLUENCE

I'm reading *The Affluent Society* in the bleachers of the ice rink while J takes a skating lesson. Another mother sits down and notices my book. Why are you reading that? she asks. I tell her that I'm trying to learn about capitalism. She asks if I think capitalism is a good thing or a bad thing. I tell her that I'm tempted to think it's a bad thing but I don't really know what it is. Or at least I don't know what it is to me, in my life and work. I'm not neutral so much as undecided. She seems slightly offended on behalf of capitalism. Her husband, she tells me, is a financial analyst. I wonder if he's any more deeply invested in capitalism than I am. Both of us live in the same affluent area, and both of us have children gliding across the ice under the same protective dome.

They're skating between road cones now and I watch the drill with some sadness. I've given up teaching J to skate myself, though I skate very well. When I laced J's skates today, I remembered my father's bare hands, ruddy in the cold, as he laced my skates in the wind on the bank of the river. He would skate backward and hold out his hands so that I could balance against him. And now here I am, paying for lessons and reading in the bleachers.

"Wealth is not without its advantages and the case to the contrary, although it has often been made, has never proved widely persuasive," John Kenneth Galbraith writes in the great first sentence of *The Affluent Society*. "But, beyond doubt, wealth is the relentless enemy of understanding."

I've made it only this far when the other mother sits down with me, but I've already read the introduction, in which Galbraith reveals that he began this book with a grant from the Guggenheim Foundation to write a study of poverty, and instead wrote a study of affluence. Nearly all people in nearly all nations, for nearly all of human history, he observes, have been poor. Widespread poverty is not an anomaly. But widespread affluence is. And if we meet this new affluence with old ideas forged in poverty, we will misunderstand ourselves.

MORAL MONDAY

Today is Moral Monday, I hear on the radio. A priest and a rabbi are staging a protest downtown with a giant camel and a giant needle, a reference to Jesus saying, "It is easier for a camel to go through the eye of a needle than for someone who is rich to enter the kingdom of God." I pause over this, wondering if money can really be so corrupting that just having it is immoral. I have my doubts, but I also have money.

Now I'm pulling weeds in the garden of the elementary school, wondering if I'm on my way to becoming an asshole. I've been reading the psychologist Paul Piff, who quotes Jesus in a paper titled "Higher Social Class Predicts Increased Unethical Behavior." Piff and his team of researchers found that the rich are more likely than the poor to cut off other vehicles when driving through intersections. And they're less likely to stop for pedestrians. They're more likely to cheat in a game, and more likely to think of greed as good. But money is not to blame for this, Piff suggests. What's to blame is the comfort that a higher class status affords—the independence, the insularity, the security, the illusion of not needing other people. "While having money doesn't necessarily make anybody anything," Piff told *New York* magazine, "the rich are way more likely to prioritize their own self-interests above the interests of other people. It makes them more likely to exhibit characteristics that we would stereotypically associate with, say, assholes."

There's a weed in this garden that's like kudzu. It's called bindweed or, less commonly, possession vine. It winds around other plants, blocking their sunlight. It's strangling the raspberries and creeping toward the arugula. It grows new roots everywhere it touches the ground and each fragment of root that I don't pull becomes another vine. It seems to have an unfair advantage over the other plants. Susie sees me working and stops to help. Did I read the article in the *Times* yesterday, she asks, about the rich?

I did. It was written by a sociologist, Rachel Sherman, who interviewed wealthy New Yorkers, people in the top 1 and 2 percent. The very rich, her study revealed, are uncomfortable with being rich. If they are assholes, they are uneasy assholes. They try to hide their spending from their nannies, cutting the tags off new clothes and peeling the labels off expensive bread. They don't boast about their wealth, but about their thrift. They talk about looking for good deals and driving old cars..

Have I told you, Susie jokes, that I drive a really old car?

It's unsettling, I agree, how similar the very rich are to us. They, too, don't admit to being rich—they are "comfortable." Like us, they budget and save and give. They tell themselves that they've worked hard. But they're ambivalent about their money and what they've bought with it. The $4 million condo seems excessive even to the people who live there. The expense is a measure of the distance between them and other people. The rich feel morally compromised, so they try to be good.

Dividing the good rich from the bad rich is a waste of time, Sherman suggests, for the rich and everyone else. "Judging wealthy people on the basis of their individual behaviors—do they work hard enough, do they consume reasonably enough, do they give back enough—distracts us from other kinds of questions about the morality of vastly unequal distributions of wealth," she writes. We shouldn't ask our rich to be good, in other words, we should ask our economic system to be better.

THE LANDLORD'S GAME

I've been playing Monopoly with J every evening for a week and I haven't won a single game. J plays with abandon, buys indiscriminately, and wins repeatedly. Tonight he's thrown a suspicious number of doubles, so I accuse him of cheating. He's not cheating, he explains to me happily, he's just a lucky person.

The Landlord's Game, the game that became Monopoly, was designed in the early 1900s to expose the problems with an economic system in which property owners "win" by impoverishing renters. The game was informed by the theories of Henry George, who proposed that profits made from a natural resource, like land or coal or oil, should be distributed equally among everyone. No individual, he argued, should build a fortune by laying claim to a collective resource. George believed that everyone was entitled to profit from their labor, but that profits made from the ownership of property should be heavily taxed.

The woman who invented the Landlord's Game, Elizabeth Magie, was an advocate of that tax. As an unmarried woman with her own home, rare at the time, she struggled to support herself on the $10 per week she earned as a stenographer. "If we could be reduced to the character of a machine," she remarked, "having only to be oiled and kept in working order, $10 perhaps would be sufficient." Rather than marry out of economic necessity, she advertised herself for sale to the highest bidder as a "young woman American slave." This made national news and caused a small scandal. Her brother, embarrassed, said she was just trying to publicize her writing. As well as being an inventor, she was also a poet.

She was trying to make a statement about women's economic dependence, Magie told reporters, and she meant only that she would sell her labor in marriage. "Of course, I am a white slave," she said, "but I am not on the block physically." Her metaphor was appreciated by Upton Sinclair, who sent money. Others were offended—not because a considerable number of people who had been enslaved were still alive and could testify that slavery was not like marriage, but because she was suggesting that marriage, like slavery, was an economic institution.

In Magie's original version of the Landlord's Game, players earned money by completing a circuit around the board and passing the square labeled "Labor upon Mother Earth Produces Wages," which is now simply "Go." Magie patented her game twice, but this didn't prevent a man, Charles Darrow, from packaging the game under the name *Monopoly* and making himself a millionaire. Parker Brothers bought Magie's patent with a onetime payment of $500, but they paid Darrow royalties for the rest of his life. Magie protested this, though the concept of earning royalties off a patent was not exactly in keeping with the philosophy of her game. "Discovery can give no right of ownership," George wrote, "for whatever is discovered must have been already here to be discovered."

Darrow took the game Magie designed, but she drew most of its distinctive features, including the continuous loop of play, from Zohn Ahl, a game played by the Kiowa people of Oklahoma. "It is bitterly ironic," writes Philip Winkelman, "that this gift of the Kiowa to America and to the world should result in the daily reenactment of the reduction of opponents to abject poverty through the parceling up and exclusive ownership of land."

No fair, J complains when I ask him for change. I owe him $450 for landing on Pennsylvania Avenue with two houses and I've given him a $500 bill. As the winning player, he is now in the habit of objecting to any transaction that involves handing money to anyone else. "Let me tell you there are no fairer-minded beings in the world than our own little American children," Magie wrote optimistically. She hoped that children who played her game would grow up understanding the injustice of our economic system. To help illustrate this injustice, she designed two sets of rules. Following one set of rules would create an equal distribution of money among players, with no winner. Following the other rules would create an accumulation of wealth, allowing one player to win. The rules that survived, the rules we still play by, are winner take all.

CAPITALISM

Dan rings our bell just to say hello. He's in the neighborhood because he's test-driving a new bike. It looks identical to John's new bike, which looks identical to John's old bike. I think I recognize that bike, I say. We all ride versions of the same bike, Dan says, laughing. He's worried that maybe he doesn't need this bike, so I tell him that I've seen John get a lot of pleasure out of a new bike. I know that Dan already has two other bikes, but I also know how much he rides. When he comes in, I ask him about capitalism. He's a sociologist, and the first person I've talked with who seems comfortable with the subject. You've read Marx? he checks. I read *Capital* in college, I tell him. And I've just read the first chapter of *Capital in the Twenty-First Century*, so I know that Piketty, like Marx, believes that capitalism, unchecked, will always produce inequality. But I still don't understand the inner workings of contemporary capitalism, the nuts and bolts of the markets, the push and pull of bubbles and recessions. Even economists, Dan says, don't understand that.

Three men won the Nobel Prize for economics in 2013, he tells me—two of them for theories that directly contradicted each other. They disagreed about bubbles, to begin with. Robert Shiller described the rapid rise of housing prices in 2005 as a bubble, and warned that prices would fall dramatically. Eugene Fama didn't think the market would produce something as silly as a bubble. Even after the housing crash, Fama denied that the housing market had been a bubble and was skeptical that bubbles existed. "I don't even know what a bubble means," he said. Economics isn't good at explaining certain things, Fama acknowledged, like what causes recessions, but he still believed that the markets were "rational." Rational markets don't make bubbles. And rational markets don't need to be regulated. Shiller, who had been tracking irrational behavior in the markets, disagreed. The idea that stock prices were rational, he wrote, was "one of the most remarkable errors in the history of economic thought."

They were on opposing sides of a major economic argument and they both won. "The prize committee," Binyamin Appelbaum reported, "said these findings showed that markets were moved by a mix of rational calculus and irrational behavior." Like us. I wonder what it means, I tell Dan, that the technical terms used to describe markets are "rational" and "irrational." It sounds like economists are debating, in sexist language, whether markets are logical men or volatile women. Markets are mathematical models, Dan says, and economics is theory. Real economic systems don't behave in accordance with theory. They are shaped by our politics and policies. "Markets are constructed by people," Appelbaum argues, "for purposes chosen by people—and people can change the rules." We don't have to privilege accumulation over distribution. But that is the rule that governs our everyday lives—our work and our play.

POKÉMON

J has two Pokémon cards that he was given on the first day of first grade by a boy who told him they were "starter cards." He doesn't know anything about Pokémon, but soon he wants more cards. At the comic book shop, we discover that a pack of these cards costs $3, which means J can buy them with the money I give him for doing chores. But what the cards cost has nothing to do with what they're worth.

The value of any given card is determined by a group of children gathered on the asphalt of the school playground. There is, in the world beyond the playground, an established market for these cards and websites that chart their rising and falling prices like stocks. But these kids don't really know about that yet. They're still inventing their own values. On the asphalt, some cards are coveted because they're shiny, others because nobody has them yet, and others because they're powerful. How powerful a card might be is divined from the numbers printed on the card, which are manipulated with flawed first-grade math that leads to debate over the exact quantity of power in play.

There's debate, too, about what constitutes a good trade. After J trades away his most powerful card for a less powerful card, I hear the babysitter asking him if he was a smart negotiator. She suggests that he might want to try to get more for a card like that next time. Then he comes home with the entire collection of another boy, two years younger, who has traded it all to him for one card.

A game can be played with these cards, supposedly, but none of the kids understand the rules. Their end is accumulation— collecting cards for a game they don't know how to play.

THE PIANO

The piano arrives with the scent of another home. This scent is not unpleasant. In fact, it smells middle class. And that is what the piano announces, once positioned in our dining room. Dada da dum—middle class! Let the lessons begin.

We got it on Craigslist! I hear J saying, in imitation of me. He doesn't know what this phrase means, but he likes it. We got it on Craigslist! he says of the sandwich I made him for lunch. We got it on Craigslist! he says of the paper airplane he has just folded for a friend.

I'm sending J to day camp for a month so that I can write. A bus picks him up and drops him off every day and the camp activities include archery and tennis. Sounds expensive, a friend observes. It is expensive, I admit, but it's an investment in my writing. I don't mean investment in the financial sense, as my writing does not reliably produce money. The work I do this summer may or may not pay for the camp.

I begin my days by practicing piano, which I do badly but with ardor. Then I read for a while. I write until I'm too hungry to keep writing and then after lunch I spend some time in my garden before writing again. I want to also study French, but I rarely do. As I meander my way through one of these days, it occurs to me that my work life resembles the life of an eighteenth-century aristocrat.

To confirm this, I consult a book on my shelf: *Men, Women, & Pianos*. It has chapter headings like "Pianos Become a Business" and "Music Becomes an Article of Commerce" and "The Piano as Furniture." The clavichords of eighteenth-century Germany, I learn, were most often played by women. "The instrument was a house furnishing, and they were mostly at home." But those women weren't expected to take their playing too seriously, or to make a career of it.

The chapter "The Piano as a Female 'Accomplishment'" explains that it was once a mark of class and prestige for a gentleman, who by definition did no manual labor, to have a wife and daughters who were idle. But "it looked more ladylike to do something uselessly pretty than to do nothing." And so, "in eighteenth- and nineteenth-century England, as well as in the rest of Europe, young feminine genteel idleness was mostly filled with a number of trivial occupations superficially related to the fine arts: they were known as 'accomplishments.'"

Both art and women were dismissed as "uselessly pretty" and "trivial." But the word that bothers me is *accomplishment*. I don't want, I think, anything to do with it. Still, I pursue it. Except at the piano, where there is no question of accomplishment. I can't play for anyone else. I've failed to learn the bass clef and I'm paralyzed by the metronome. Reading the notation takes everything I have and just eight measures of "Frère Jacques" breaks me. But there, in the break, is a moment of communion between the music and me. This is practice. And practice is all I want out of art.

ART

The man sitting next to him at the café this morning caught John's attention. There was something about the way he moved that seemed familiar. As John was noticing this, the man turned to him and offered him some coupons for free pizza. Are you by any chance from the South Side? John asked. He was. In fact, he grew up a few blocks from where John grew up.

This has happened before, when John saw the mother of the new kid at school standing on the other side of the playground and declared with certainty that she was from the South Side, which she was. And when he said hello to the man who lives in the house with the "Proud Union Home" sign on the porch, and the man invited him up for a beer, having recognized that John, too, is from the South Side. Class is like race in this way, John says, it's written on your body. But I can't see it, so I don't know how to read it.

The man in the café had done some work for the pizza shop next door and they'd given him the coupons. His work? He was a private investigator. He gave John his card, which pictured a handsome man, maybe him, looking through binoculars. "James Joyce," the card read, "Private Investigator." About 60 percent of his work involved marital disputes, he said. But he would do anything. Last week, he had gone undercover as a woman.

A hustler, John says to me now. All us South Siders are hustlers. He says this with pride and something else, maybe chagrin. I remember my suspicion, when I first met John, that he was a confidence man. The coupons, I notice, expire today.

All artists are hustlers, my mother used to say. We have to be. This was an essential part of my education as an artist. As was "The Dead" by James Joyce.

WORK

I meet Connie at the bookstore and we talk about how little we've been getting done. I've just been staring at a blank page, I tell her, and sometimes swimming in the lake. My work right now consists mostly of thinking and rethinking. I erase nearly everything I write. As I work, I pass through a predictable cycle of confusion, frustration, and despair, reaching the end of every day feeling thoroughly debased, with nothing on the page. I report all this with amazement, because I know, as Connie does, that something will come of this nothingness. The cashier is listening to us. She sells the books we write and she brings some to the register for us to sign while we continue to talk about our days of doing nothing.

That ain't workin', I think, *that's the way you do it*. These lyrics used to puzzle me, back in the eighties when I was a kid and MTV was new. I didn't know that Mark Knopfler was singing in character, and that he wrote that song in an appliance store. He was standing in front of a wall of televisions all tuned to MTV, talking with a man in work boots who was delivering boxes. He wrote down what the man said and, as Knopfler explained, "He's singing the song."

In Knopfler's mind the deliveryman was singing the song, but Knopfler was onstage and it was Knopfler who got a letter from the editor of a gay newspaper. Less than a year after the song came out, he was singing *see the little queenie* instead of *see the little faggot*. He told *Rolling Stone*, "The singer in 'Money for Nothing' is a real ignoramus, hardhat mentality—somebody who sees everything in financial terms. I mean, this guy has a grudging respect for rock stars. He sees it in terms of, well, that's not working and yet the guy's rich; that's a good scam."

The musician breaks the rules of work by playing, rather than working. It's queer, in that it's a transgression. Maybe that's what Knopfler meant when he called the rock star a faggot while singing as the deliveryman. Or maybe he was just off-loading his own bigotry onto a working-class avatar. Maybe the deliveryman was him, after all.

Long before "Money for Nothing," Knopfler recorded a demo of "In the Gallery," which he wrote in a car after walking through a gallery in London. He wasn't a rock star yet—he was working as a teacher and sleeping on the floor of his brother's apartment. The gallery was full of piles of bricks and trash being sold as art. Knopfler performed "In the Gallery" as himself, singing: *And then you get an artist says he doesn't want to*

paint at all / He takes an empty canvas and sticks it on the wall.
Money for nothing.

In the logic of the MTV video, the faggot in question is Knopfler. The singer, the deliveryman, is watching him perform.
Real video footage of the real Knopfler appears on the TV
screens in the appliance store. Meanwhile, the deliveryman is
doing real work but he is not real—he is computer animated.

None of this, John points out, would be interesting if Knopfler weren't a real artist and a great guitarist. He didn't want
to do the video for "Money for Nothing," the video that made
the song a hit. The director said, "The problem was that Mark
Knopfler was very anti-videos. All he wanted to do was perform, and he thought that videos would destroy the purity of
songwriters and performers." Because MTV, like the deliveryman, was moving merchandise.

The opening line of the song, *I want my MTV,* was sung by
Sting. It was a marketing slogan repurposed as art mocking
marketing, delivered by a millionaire musician. Sting sang that
line when he stopped by the studio in the Caribbean where
Dire Straits were recording "Money for Nothing." He had been
windsurfing nearby.

All the musicians I know who aren't rich, which is most of
them, seem to be living working-class lives. Except for the
fact that they travel all the time. But I don't know what de-

fines a working-class life. Is it the way you live, or the amount of money you make, or the nature of your work? John doesn't like the term. He rarely uses it. *Trash* is what he calls his own background. Has anyone ever suggested, he once asked me, as a means of making the suggestion, that the word *class* doesn't mean anything?

ANYTHING

What I understand, after reading a book called *Understanding Class*, is that class is hard to understand. Nobody agrees on what it is, not even the people who study it. There are no classes—class is dead. Or there are hundreds of classes, and each occupation constitutes its own class. But workers in different occupations share common concerns, Erik Olin Wright argues. Teachers, nurses, janitors, police officers, firefighters, and clerical workers all came together in Wisconsin in 2011 to protest legislation that would end their ability to unionize. And reports of the death of class, which was announced during the economic prosperity of the 1990s, were greatly exaggerated. "Class boundaries," Wright insists, "especially the property boundary, continue to constitute real barriers in people's lives."

The barriers that prevent people from entering the middle class are the defining feature of the middle class, according to one way of thinking about class. While members of the middle class acquire education and skills, for instance, we exclude others from acquiring education and skills. *Opportunity hoarding* is the term for this, and it takes the form of admissions procedures, testing, tuition costs, licensing, ranking, and all sorts of credentialing. Conveniently, we don't tend to think of these barriers as a means of protecting our class status, but as necessary measures to gauge intelligence or ability or commitment or excellence or hard work.

And then there is the Marxist approach to class, which focuses on how economic status gives some people control over the lives of others. The middle class, in this approach, lies between the capitalists who have control and the workers who are controlled. The middle class includes small-business owners who are both capitalists and workers, salaried managers and supervisors whose financial interests are entangled with the corporations they serve, and educated professionals who have enough capital to make investments. This is a middle class with capitalist aspirations. And that is why Marx considered this class dangerous. It is a class of conflicting allegiances and internal contradictions.

Most people, Wright observes, prefer not to think of class as a means of control or exclusion, but as a collection of things that can be acquired, like property and education. Your class, in this approach, is determined by how much you have of three kinds of capital—economic capital, cultural capital, and social capital. Or, what you own, what you know, and who you know.

The Great British Class Survey of 2013 asked more than a hundred thousand people about their income and property, how they spent their leisure time, and the occupations of their friends. The results identified seven distinct classes. At the top were the elite, who had the most of all three kinds of capital, and at the bottom were the precariat, who had the least of everything. In between were three varieties of middle class, along with two different working classes.

"All sides played Spot the Fake Accent," Michael Goldfarb writes of his time at Oxford in the seventies, "whether it was the grammar school boy mocking the toff playing at being one of the ordinary lads, or the first generation middle-class kid being satirized for trying to sound posh." It was family background, more than income, that determined class then, he notes. But the game has changed. And now there is more economic mobility in Britain than there is in the United States. Most of the mobility in the US happens within the middle classes, where people move up and down by gradations, while the poor tend to stay poor and the rich tend to stay rich.

I enter my income and the value of my home into the Great British Class Calculator on the BBC website and check boxes to indicate that I listen to indie rock and hip-hop and visit museums and have friends who are artists and professors and scientists. I'm in the elite, the survey reveals. But that's before I adjust my income to pounds from dollars, which puts me in the established middle class. I'm just an exchange rate away from the elite. According to the survey, I have passed through several classes in my adult life, including the precariat. But I don't believe that to be true. I have always remained, more or less, in the class into which I was born.

In his heart, John tells me, he's trash. It's what he comes from and it's what he is. But he knows that he doesn't live like trash. He's gone from a childhood on the South Side to an adulthood on the North Side. John's father worked in a factory and didn't go to college. His family owned a house, like mine. And both of our mothers didn't have their own income until they left our fathers. Our mothers weren't in the same class, exactly, but they were in the same boat.

The economic lives of an entire generation of Americans, all nearly my age, have been tracked by researchers who just released their findings, which I'm reading about in the *New York Times*. An animated chart illustrates the fate of fifty thousand white children, girls and boys, from different income levels. Five streams run parallel in this chart, one for each level of income, and the children are little square boats carried along on their parents' income. Then, at adulthood, all the streams meet and cross in a muddle where some children float into higher incomes while others float down. More boys are heading upstream and more girls are carried downstream, passing each other in between incomes. This chart doesn't look as much like a waterway now as it does a machine. It's a series of conveyor belts carrying children, sorting them, then sending them up or down. And it looks like it's designed to make those girls fall.

Another chart illustrates what became of fifty thousand boys, white and black, who grew up poor. The boys are color-coded squares that travel through a crowded pipeline until they emerge out the other end, where most of them continue at ground level to become poor adults, though many white boys miraculously ascend, flying up to higher incomes. The next chart tracks fifty thousand boys who grew up rich. They are carried along a stream that splits off into four tributaries: upper-middle class, middle class, lower-middle class, poor. As I watch, many of the white boys continue to float along the rich stream while more of the black boys are carried away, falling down a waterfall into the lower tributaries.

There are more charts, more pipelines, more dizzying machines. Black children and Native American children fall. Hispanic children fall, but not as far. Asian American and white children are more likely to rise. These charts track only income, not other dimensions of class. And they don't illustrate, because this isn't in the data, what the children carry with them as they rise or fall. There's no measure of how they're marked by their background, in the way they talk or what they value or how they think about money and risk and security. And there's no evidence, once they've arrived at a new income, of who they believe themselves to be.

I return to *Understanding Class*, which I left open to a poster from the seventies that pictures a woman with a cleaning rag leaning against a fence, deep in thought. Across the top is written: "Class consciousness is knowing which side of the fence you're on."

PASSING

I'm putting away the silverware John has just washed. It isn't silver, it's steel, and it isn't really ours. It was given to me in graduate school by a friend who tried to get it back and I still consider it hers. My friend was newly married when I met her and the silverware was from her registry. I owned, at the time, two spoons and a knife from a thrift store. I'd forgone forks to afford two glasses and I'd never heard of a registry. My friend told me that her silverware had rusted in the dishwasher and she'd need a new set. She couldn't return this set, so she gave it to me, as I didn't have silverware or a dishwasher. Then my friend learned at the department store that all she had to do to restore her silverware was what I had done, rub it with a cloth. She told me this in hopes that I would be moved to give back the silverware. But I wasn't moved. She had a house with curtains and a toaster and a set of matching dishes—all things I considered luxuries.

My friend was deeply in debt, I know now, paying a mortgage and deferring her undergraduate loans while she lived off her graduate loans. When I took her silverware, I was feeding off her debt. I had only two spoons because my loans were much smaller than hers. I borrowed as little as possible in graduate school and bought almost nothing. It wasn't moral, my aversion to credit. I just couldn't foresee a future when I'd be able to pay anything back. I didn't think I would ever make any money as an artist. Credit is a form of optimism, Yuval Noah Harari suggests. It depends on the belief that the future will be more prosperous than the present.

I kept the silverware because I couldn't tell the difference between credit and wealth. If I had a better eye for class, I would have seen that I was surrounded by people subsisting on credit, living precariously and passing as middle class. Credit creates the illusion of equality, in that we can all buy the same things on credit, but we can't all pay the debt back.

"The Inescapable Weight of my $100,000 Student Debt" is the headline under which the writer M. H. Miller tells the story of his loans. He was at New York University on his way to a graduate degree when his father lost his job at an auto parts supplier for Ford. The mortgage on Miller's childhood home went into default. By the time he graduated, with a BA and an MA in English and a journal full of notes on Virginia Woolf, the house had been lost to the bank and his mother had been diagnosed with cancer. His parents declared bankruptcy and their car was repossessed. In his first years of working in New York, Miller's debt seemed so impossible to repay that he fantasized about dying. Now he works as an editor at the *New York Times*, but he makes less than he owes and he lives paycheck to paycheck.

Marx, too, was dogged by debt, by doctor's bills and butcher's bills and unpaid rent. He lived beyond his means, without a credit card. He pawned his wife's linens and silver, and he pawned his own overcoat. He would redeem the overcoat when he needed to do research at the British Library, where a coat was required, and then pawn it again when he needed money. Engels sent money regularly and Marx asked him to send more. Eventually, Engels supported them both by selling his share in his father's factory. When Marx got an inheritance, he moved into a large house. Shortly after, he wrote to Engels that he had spent £500, the equivalent of a sizable annual salary today, paying off debts and furnishing the house, and now he needed money to pay the landlord.

Marx would not work as a "wage slave," and he saw what this would mean for his daughters. They would have to marry well or become servants. So Marx pretended at a bourgeois life. His girls were given lessons in art and riding and music, and they hosted a ball in the new house. All this, Marx wrote to Engels, was in the interest of "securing their future." A proletarian life would be quite all right for him, he insisted, "if the girls were boys."

Speaking of passing, Robyn says, at the former girls' school where she went to college there was a special fund for students on financial aid. This fund was established by a private donor to help pay for the things a student without money might need to pass among her moneyed friends. The description of the fund, long outdated, suggested that a student might apply for funding if, for example, she had been invited to the opera but she didn't have the proper gloves. Robyn used the fund to visit museums, though she would also have liked the proper gloves.

MEMBERSHIP

Athena! J shouts as he approaches the statue. It is indeed a bust of Athena. He recognized her by her helmet. You have so much, John says quietly, almost under his breath. You know so many things that I didn't know when I was your age, you know who Athena is, he says. J has run deeper into antiquities and isn't listening to him, but I am.

John sold used cars, worked construction, and bought himself a one-way ticket to Paris before he wandered through the museums where he learned about Athena. J gets his classics delivered to him at bedtime, just as I did. But still, I think I know something of what John is feeling.

Weren't there any women in the twentieth century? John is asking now. We're walking through the modern wing, where every painting we've passed so far was made by a man. Upstairs, I laugh out loud in front of *Venus de Milo with Drawers*. I've never seen it before, never been to this floor of the Art Institute. This Venus has a drawer with a fuzzy pull in the middle of her forehead. She's been made into furniture, which of course she already was.

John has a beer in the museum café and I drink sparkling water from a cobalt-blue bottle. I wanted the bottle more than the water. John is pensive. I can't come here without thinking about money, he says, the whole experience just seems saturated with money. Museums in Europe never made him feel this way. What's the difference? He's not sure. The people, he gestures toward a couple who are wearing geometric jackets that announce themselves as art not clothes. And the names everywhere, he says, reminding us who paid for this.

On our way out, I buy a membership.

ART

David is over for dinner and we're talking about art, the kind you hang on your walls. We've been in this house for a year and we still don't have anything on the walls. In our apartment, we had a drawing I made tacked to our living room wall with masking tape. I joked that it was a $20,000 crayon drawing, because that was how much the year that I studied drawing and painting in college cost. But I didn't pay for that year, or the next three, myself.

After college, when I was paying for my life, I had only a bed in my apartment. But I had art on my walls. I got the art from a friend who traded it to me for a book that I had bound myself. Artists like her were expected to make their work on acid-free paper, using only archival materials. In rebellion, she made her drawings on paper she soaked in coffee and bathed in acid. One of them was in the rough shape of a house, stained with black tea, its boards held together with thread stitched by hand. I still have it, but it's fading and falling apart, as she intended.

Now that we have money, I say, maybe we should buy some art. We should put our money into the pockets of artists. I'm trying out this idea, but I'm not committed to it. I know less about buying art than I do about buying furniture. Art, for me, has always been a thing to do, not a thing to buy. The art that is sold in galleries seems to belong to another world entirely. The art world.

John says he's not sure that I can say we have money. David, who has just finished paying off his credit card debt, is following this argument with interest. When the Occupy movement was still making headlines, I tell them, I learned that 75 percent of the households in Chicago made less than ours. We were in the top 25 percent, and that was before I got the raise that brought my salary up to $73,000, making our household income $125,000.

We had money, John concedes, but we spent it on this house. Now we live in our money.

Yes, I agree, with no art.

POOR

The babysitter reports that last week J asked her if she was poor and she said yes, but then she felt wrong about her answer all week. I didn't want him to think this is what it looks like to be poor, she says, gesturing toward her North Face coat and her L.L.Bean backpack. The babysitter is a former student of mine who worked all through college, unlike most of my students. This week J asked her again if she was poor and she said no. So, you're rich, he said. Well, it's all relative, she said.

J was feeling rich because David had given us a tall candle, the tallest candle J had ever seen. It was a votive candle meant to bring abundance into our lives. How much more abundance, I wondered, could we absorb? I was feeling rich, too.

After the babysitter explained what *relative* meant, J said, I have a really tall candle, but someone else might have a taller candle than mine, so they're rich and I'm not?

This, I tell the babysitter, is why nobody thinks they're rich.

RICH

I'm compiling evidence that we're rich, I text to John. We're still having this argument, but it's a play fight. I'm in New York, where all my friends have moved farther from the center of the city since I last visited. Their rents keep going up. Standing in their apartments, I can feel the cost of living. Less money buys more in Chicago, which makes me feel rich here. But the price of feeling rich, in this case, is not living in New York.

One definition of what it means to be rich, which is not mine, is to have a household income over twice the median income where you live. In Chicago, that's anything over $136,806. In New York, it's anything over $150,736. I suspect that is not nearly enough to feel rich in New York. But as Elizabeth Chin writes, "Not feeling rich and elite does not mean it is not so."

Molly shows me the Murphy bed that folds down from the wall in her new apartment. I'll sleep here tonight and wake up to the gasp of a bus stopping outside the window. Tomorrow we'll ride a train for two hours and walk to the queer beach at Far Rockaway, by the bathhouses boarded over with plywood. "A monument to Art Deco design, grand public works and populist fun," the *New York Times* called those once-glorious bathhouses, which were left half-renovated after funding ran out. The superintendent of the park explained, "We have to spread the wealth around, or the lack of wealth."

When Molly's father died suddenly she inherited his apartment on Madison Avenue, where she and I lived for a summer while she tried to figure out what to do with his property. We slept together in her dead father's bed and marveled at the contents of his kitchen cupboards. There were many jars of capers and neither of us knew what they were. We tasted them and decided they were inedible. Now those capers were hers, along with a glass display cabinet and a heavily framed print of Käthe Kollwitz's *Woman with Dead Child*. Not anything she wanted.

She didn't want her inheritance, the property or the money. She didn't want to become the person that having money might make her—she wanted to stay in the fray. So she gave her inheritance away, I think. We haven't talked about it for years but I can see how she lives. She has less space than I do, and fewer things, and she spends more hours at her job than I spend teaching. Yes, she's living off her salary, she tells me now. But she still has her inheritance. Or most of it. She has given large sums away. And she still intends to give it all away—just as much as she did twenty years ago.

Now she's back where she grew up, not the apartment on Madison Avenue, but the Dominican neighborhood with bodegas and little hardware stores. Laundry lines are strung across the ceiling of her apartment, and pots and pans hang in the window. There's a new desk from IKEA in the living room, which is also the office and the dining room. She surveys the room with me. So, she says, is this what we do now? We just keep earning money and replacing this stuff with better stuff?

In her father's apartment, on the table next to his bed, was a bowl of beautiful glass cherries. I secretly coveted them. Molly found them ridiculous, and emblematic of wealth—fruit that can't be eaten.

WORK

LEISURE

You should look into the etymology of *scholastic*, Vojislav suggests. I can't imagine why. We're talking about work, about my job at the university. It's from the Greek, he says, and it means "to be at leisure to study." The Greeks didn't value work like we do—work was for slaves and women—but they did value study. The word he wants to call my attention to, I know, is *leisure*.

Leisure meant something different in ancient Greece. It was the opposite of being busy but it wasn't rest or play. It was time spent on reflective thought and wonder. To be at leisure, to live a life of study and contemplation, was to enjoy true freedom. But that freedom depended on the work of women and slaves. And, as Aristotle remarked, "There is no leisure for slaves."

When time is money, as it is now, free time is never free. It's expensive. In *The Theory of the Leisure Class*, Thorstein

Veblen writes that leisure is a form of conspicuous consumption, with time being what is consumed. The upper class is exempt from ordinary employment under capitalism, he observes, just as the aristocracy is exempt from manual labor under feudalism. Leisure is how a class that doesn't have to work displays its status.

We no longer have a leisure class in America, Galbraith argues in *The Affluent Society*. Our rich work, or at least act busy. While leisure has gone out of fashion, a new class has emerged—a class of people who don't work for money. They are paid, but payment is not the point. They work for a sense of fulfillment, for the rewards of the work itself. Pay is incidental, though it serves, Galbraith notes, as an "index of prestige." And prestige, along with respect, is a source of satisfaction for the members of this class. They like to be well paid, but the suggestion that they are motivated by money would insult them. "Such is the labor of the New Class," Galbraith writes. "No aristocrat ever contemplated the loss of feudal privileges with more sorrow than a member of this class would regard his descent into ordinary labor where the reward was only the pay."

I flush when I read this—I feel found out. And I read the entire chapter again before I understand that Galbraith considers the New Class a promising development. The goal of an affluent society, he suggests, should be to continue reducing the number of people engaged in work *qua* work. The hours in a standard workweek should be reduced, too. And the New Class should be spending some of their pleasurable work hours, he argues, thinking of ways to make work more pleasurable for everyone.

I call Robyn to tell her about the New Class, an addendum to the letter I just sent, also about class. She doesn't know if my letter arrived because she doesn't want her neighbors to see her walking out to the mailbox at noon, which is when the mail is delivered. Her neighbors have a protestant work ethic and nine-to-five lives. She'll have to wait until five to check the mail, she laughs. She's on sabbatical, writing a book. But her neighbors don't know this. She doesn't want them to think she isn't working.

THE PROTESTANT ETHIC

Maggie has a new house with a pool and I've been swimming in it all day. Now I'm leaning on her kitchen counter eating chocolate and talking about work. I once told Maggie that I had a protestant work ethic. That was when I was taking care of her son. The *protestant ethic* was the name I gave to my insistence on continuing to try to put him to bed even after she had come home from work and could lie down next to him herself. It was a strange favor to impose on a friend, this refusal to give up bedtime duty. We laughed about it then—I just wanted to do a good job. That's my ethic, though it is not, as I've come to understand, the protestant ethic.

Max Weber published *The Protestant Ethic and the Spirit of Capitalism* in 1905, during his recovery from a breakdown that interrupted his ability to work. He couldn't teach, but he recovered sufficiently to write a book in which he asks why, if greed is as old as time, did modern capitalism emerge in northern Europe during the seventeenth century? He wasn't the first to ask this question, Elizabeth Kolbert notes, and he wouldn't be the last. "But," she writes, "the answer he came up with—in effect, that Donald Trump is the spiritual heir of Martin Luther—probably still ranks as the most perverse."

Weber proposed that early Protestants believed they must work to accumulate wealth as proof that they were in God's favor. This was a departure from the Catholic notion of good works—service done for others to earn salvation. Capitalism couldn't really take hold, Weber noted, until people became convinced, one way or another, to make more money than they needed. That would seem an easy sell today, but it wasn't in seventeenth-century England, when many commoners still earned money only occasionally, lived mostly by subsistence, and felt that they had enough, much to the frustration of the landowners who wanted them to do steady work for wages. "A man does not 'by nature' wish to earn more and more money," Weber argues, "but simply to live as he is accustomed to live and to earn as much as is necessary for that purpose."

The *protestant ethic* describes the moralizing of work and the privileging of property, not, as I used to think, the belief that work is, in and of itself, good. All this time I've been using that term to describe my faith in work. Being neither Protestant nor Catholic, I've absorbed my ideas about work from the atmosphere. And I've believed, for most of my life, that work is good.

WORK

I'm out for drinks with a friend from work who tells me, after our second cocktail, that my comments have been redacted from the Program Report. I say that I hope they put thick black lines through them, like in an FBI file. No, she says, it didn't happen like that. My comments were just erased—there is a blank where I noted that the structure of the program allows the bosses to ignore the concerns of the lowest-ranking teachers, most of us women. There is also a blank where I detailed the small abuses enabled by that structure—the everyday condescension, the extraction of labor, and the occasional coercion. The redaction had to happen, my colleague explains, because my complaint was actionable. Meaning, it seems, that if it had not been erased then something would have to be done about it.

I always liked it, work. At least at first. Pushing a broom across the concrete floor at the farm where I punched my first time card, running the register at a vegetable stand, assembling cabbage boxes behind a greenhouse. Reading "Bartleby the Scrivener" aloud to the mystified children of a summer camp. Standing naked in front of a classroom of art students. That was good work, and not just because it paid $10 an hour. I was in college then and I enjoyed standing still, thinking. And I loved, myself, drawing nudes. I knew what a service it was to have a body to draw from, and I preferred work that felt like service.

There was another model who worked with me sometimes, a man who was nearly ninety. During the summers, he and his wife traveled around the country in their RV, visiting museums where he studied the masters. Not to learn to paint or sculpt, but to learn the poses. He was the carpenter's hammer, he told me, or the nail. He had a binder full of Polaroids of the poses he had mastered. There he was, an ancient *David*, a wizened *Augustus*, a grizzled *Thinker*.

I found an ad that offered $20 an hour for an artist's model, so I drove to a warehouse by the river and took a freight elevator to the top floor. The man who met me at the elevator was a photographer who sold his work to magazines. He liked to shoot naked women in cemeteries, he told me, on graves. I should have left then, but I had already taken off my clothes. He asked if I would mind lying down on the floor and opening my legs. How could I not have known this was coming? I was surprised, naively, to find my body in service to necrophilic pornography. I know now that this is how it is with work—sometimes the contract is revised while you're on the job, already undressed.

CAPITALISM

At a dinner for work I'm sitting between a botanist and an economist and we're talking about kudzu. This isn't work, but it isn't leisure either. The economist mentions the Pigouvian tax, a tax that's added to the price of a thing because of the social cost of that thing. Like the tax on cigarettes. How would one calculate the tax, the economist muses, on an invasive plant like kudzu? How much should it cost if someone wanted to plant it in their garden?

As he says this, I'm thinking that if the price of every item reflected its social cost, then a lot of things should be much more expensive—bottled water, online shopping, bullets. The social cost of some things is their very cheapness. Chicken McNuggets, made cheap at the expense of the birds, bred so that they can barely walk, and at the expense of the workers, who gut and cut them on factory lines moving at the rate of forty birds per minute. We will eventually be buried with those chickens. "The fossilized trace of a trillion birds will outlast—and mark the passage of—the humans who made them," Raj Patel and Jason Moore write in *A History of the World in Seven Cheap Things*. What about capitalism, I wonder, could we tax capitalism itself?

I ask the economist if he can explain to me what capitalism is. The botanist leaves to get a drink. Capital, he begins, is a means of production. That much I already know. And capitalism is a system in which one builds wealth by owning a means of production. Like a factory, he says, or a cow.

Or land? I ask. Yes, land. Or another person. Even a sharpened stick is capital. Capitalism has been around a long time, he says, it's as old as ownership.

I think he's wrong on this, but we're talking about fossil fuels now. Oil and coal are capital, he says, and we need to leave that capital in the ground. We should not mine it, sell it, buy it, or burn it. But people already own it. A journalist recently observed, he says, that the last time we walked away from an accumulation of capital this significant was Emancipation.

LIBERATION COLLECTION

They Were Her Property is sitting next to my bed, waiting to be read. I've opened it to the front flap, which tells me: "Because women typically inherited more slaves than land, enslaved people were often their primary source of wealth. . . . White women actively participated in the slave market, profited from it, and used it for economic and social empowerment." I'm having trouble getting past this to the first page. I close the book and look at the picture on the front, a well-dressed white woman raising her hand at an auction to bid on a bare-breasted black woman.

Enslaved people were a kind of property that white women could continue to own and control even after they were married. Slavery is what allowed those married women to fully participate in capitalism. They were eager participants—buying slaves themselves, negotiating aggressively, and selling other women's children. Stephanie Jones-Rogers calls them "mistresses of the market." They were mistresses, she clarifies, in the original sense of the word. In this sense, *mistress* was the equivalent of *master*, and it meant "a woman who hath something in possession."

If commodities could speak, Marx imagined that they would discuss their own value as objects. Teacups maybe, full of tea, comparing their relative value to the teapot. Imagine instead, Fred Moten writes, a recording that captures the shrieks of Frederick Douglass's Aunt Hester as she hangs from her tied wrists on a hook in the kitchen, lashed by her owner for giving herself to someone else. Imagine her testament, turning and turning on a record player. Remember that "the object resists, the commodity shrieks, the audience participates."

I'm in the audience, reading newspaper stories about the Confederate monuments that have been toppled in the night. Ben calls to tell me about the story he's reporting. He's just interviewed Dora Robinson, a black woman who keeps a collection of mammies in her home. Her liberation collection, she calls it. At the center of the collection is Aunt Jemima, a heavy cast-iron doorstop, black with a white apron. Robinson found Aunt Jemima at a yard sale, where the white woman who owned her wanted $100, which was too much. Robinson drove away, but then she had to go back for Aunt Jemima. She took possession of her to liberate her.

As a child I collected empty syrup bottles, each in the form of a woman. They were Mrs. Butterworth's bottles, sold now on eBay as Aunt Jemima bottles. Mrs. Butterworth and Aunt

Jemima both serve breakfast, and they both wear aprons. But Mrs. Butterworth goes by her last name. *The Peoples News*, a satirical newspaper, reports that DNA evidence has revealed what I already suspected: "Butterworth is white, but has spent the last 45 years passing." And, "She said she never would have become such a success had she been white." Success, in her line of work, is best performed by a person who can pass as an object.

I kept the bottles in a sticky row on a bookshelf. They were my beautiful things, saved from the trash. I wanted to possess them, and maybe to liberate them. I was intrigued, as a child, that a bottle could also be a woman. She had a job, this woman, holding syrup. But when it was all poured out, when she was empty and her job was done, she became something else.

WORK

I'm afraid to admit, even to myself, that I don't want to work. But after one glass of wine I'm confessing to Vojislav. He shrugs, of course I want to quit my job. He'd like to quit his job, too. I would still have plenty of work, I say, even without my job. I would have the work of writing, the work of research, housework and yard work, and the work of caring for a child. Work, in fact, is interfering with my work, and I want to work less so that I can have more time to work. I need another word.

Work, Lewis Hyde writes, is distinct from labor. Work is something we do by the hour, and labor sets its own pace. Work, if we are fortunate, is rewarded with money, but the reward for labor is transformation. "Writing a poem," Hyde writes, "raising a child, developing a new calculus, resolving a neurosis, invention in all forms—these are labors." This list reveals to me my problem. I want to give my life to labor, not work.

Or the other way around. The meanings of *labor* and *work* are reversed in Andrea Komlosy's *Work: The Last 1,000 Years*. Both words can be traced back to Latin, she writes, which gave every Indo-European language two words for work. In Latin, *labor* meant arduous toil, and the word *laborare* came from the swaying of slaves under heavy loads. *Opus*, which became our *work*, was creative and productive. This work was satisfying, a source of pleasure and a sense of accomplishment.

There is a blurring of meanings now, in many languages, between the words for arduous toil and satisfying work. In everyday English, a laborer is a worker and labor is work, except in childbirth. In contemporary German, *werk* is no longer a euphemism for sex. But *werk* can mean pain, and *sie hat ihre werke* can be said of a menstruating woman—she is having her works. The range of words for work was more expansive, Komlosy notes, before work came to be defined by paid employment in the nineteenth century. "Much of what once was assumed to be work was later excluded from the category as it became increasingly focused on gainful employment."

Many jobs demand both work and labor, in Hyde's sense. The labor of teaching, which I love for its transformative power, is accompanied by ordinary paperwork and the work of being an employee, which is more toilsome than the work of teaching. Bureaucracies have a way of making work out of labor and—as I observed on parents' night, when J's kindergarten teacher listed the corporations that supplied her with branded coursework—a teacher can be robbed of her labor and left with mostly work.

This, I guess, is what Marx meant by workers alienated from their labor. That phrase didn't mean much to me when I read *Capital* twenty years ago, but now it does.

DRAG

The hardest part of working isn't the work, my mother tells me, it's the passing. She means passing as an office worker—dressing the part, performing the rituals of office life, and acting appropriately grateful for a ten-hour shift at a computer. After a lifetime of working, mostly at things that didn't earn money, she now has an office job. Her boss keeps reminding her to work faster and make fewer mistakes. It's a drag.

"Executive" was one of the categories of competition in the drag balls of *Paris Is Burning*. Executive drag involved wearing the clothes and walking the walk of money and power. It combined the practicality of passing with the play of drag. Trophies were awarded for "realness," but this was a realness laced with irony, as the black drag queens of the eighties ball scene were twice removed from any opportunity to pass as executives. Some of them didn't have anywhere to live and some were hustling for money, doing sex work to pay the bills. One said, "A ball, to us, is as close to reality as we're gonna get to all of that fame and fortune and stardom and spotlights."

RuPaul was sleeping on couches in New York and storing his belongings in the basement of the Pyramid Club while Paris was burning. I watch the video for his first hit, where he plays a supermodel who grew up poor. Acting out a fantasy of making it big, a fantasy very much like his real life, he works his way through powders, mascaras, lipsticks, feather boas, satin gloves, statement necklaces, silk scarves, and stiletto heels to a wild-eyed finale. *You better work*, he sings. *Work it girl*. And again, *Work*. Wink. *Work*.

That was long before his drag race. Now he wears pink suits with secret stitching inside that reads: "YOU'RE BORN NAKED AND THE REST IS DRAG." We're all performing, he wants us to know, but some of us are following the script more closely than others, and some of us have been given easier parts. Easier parts with better pay.

Doing drag is an act of treason, he tells a journalist. Drag, he tells another journalist, is his way of saying f-you to a male-dominated culture. And so, I wonder, who is he working for? For himself? For liberation? For the women whose clothes he has revealed as costumes, the wearing of which is a kind of work?

Now I'm listening to Rihanna: *Work, work, work, work, work, work.* Her song hints at the drudgery of making hit after hit. And the ordinary work of performing sex appeal on and off the job. The video is understated, dim and smoky. A working-class after-work scene. It's an anti-video, in that it's not glamorizing. The song is from the album *Anti*, along with songs about embezzlement and the American dream. "Work" is magnetic and repetitive. "It doesn't really go anywhere," Spencer Kornhaber writes of the song. "It approximates what work feels like." The chorus shifts from *work* to *dirt* to *work* to *learn* to *tired.*

It sounds like life on a kibbutz, Robyn says. Yes, I laugh, like a day in my garden. And then Drake steps in and says, *Yeah, okay you need to get done, done, done, done.*

I'm done with work for today and I walk to dinner with friends from work. The video for "Work" is still on my mind, the second video, the one shot in a pink living room. If the song is about the work of love, the ongoing effort of making it work while still showing up for work, the video is about the work of sex. The grind of grinding. The soft monotony, the slow rise of a sweat. Rihanna dances for Drake, and then he dances for her. It's seductive, in a workaday way.

She's either bringing sex to work, I say, or putting work into sex.

No, Michelle argues, she's saying, *You have to work for me.* It's a power play.

Work, Jim sings, à la RuPaul.

If she's playing with power, I think, she seems somewhat bored of the game.

Work, Jim sings.

THE WITCH

Baba Yaga, J says, out of nowhere.

I can't get away from Baba Yaga. She's one of the witches of my childhood, and the only one who truly frightened me. In the stories my mother told, she lived in a house that stood on chicken feet and her door was locked with clenched teeth. A fence of skulls surrounded her house and when the sun set the eyes of the skulls glowed with embers.

Baba Yaga followed me when I left home, appearing in my first semester of college. I was taking a class on Russian literature and I couldn't appreciate Pushkin, my professor insisted, without knowing Russian folklore. I was surprised to discover that Baba Yaga was literature, not just a witch my mother had conjured. Baba Yaga was a woman of contradictions, I learned. She tried to burn girls alive but she also gave them powers.

The professor herself, we joked, was a witch. She was old, with deep-set eyes, two dark sockets. But her hair was the long, lush hair of a younger woman. She had written a book, *Mother Russia: The Feminine Myth in Russian Culture*, and she was full of fairy tales. It was a source of great hilarity what she told us about the witch's broomstick, that it symbolized a penis. In some tales, she said, witches rode not broomsticks, but men. And back in the time when those tales were told, a man who woke in the morning aching or sweaty might say that a witch had been riding him.

She hoped I would continue to study literature, the professor told me at the end of the course. She had taken me aside to tell me this, as if she knew something about me that I did not yet know. I found it funny that she thought I had an inclination for the sort of work that involved seeing a broomstick as a penis, but now here I am, reading *Caliban and the Witch*, underlining: "the myth of the old witch flying on her broom . . . was the projection of an extended penis, symbol of an unbridled lust."

The witch hunts in Europe reached their peak as slave ships sailed to the Americas and feudal relations gave way to capitalism. The burning of women, the enslavement of Africans, and the theft of indigenous land were all, Silvia Federici suggests, part of the same process. Capitalism, she writes, has always depended on theft and violence.

"Crossing all boundaries, the witch-hunt spread from France and Italy to Germany, Switzerland, England, Scotland, and

Sweden," Federici writes. The church urged secular authori-
ties to find and punish witches, governments declared witch-
craft a capital crime, and the newly invented printing press
was put to work publicizing witch trials. Thousands of women
were tried, stripped and shaved, tortured with needles, hanged,
and burned. The witch hunts, Federici argues, weren't about
superstition or religion so much as they were about suppress-
ing the rebellions of women.

In feudal Europe, peasant women lived under the authority of
a lord, who claimed possession of them. But they had a kind
of economic power that women wouldn't have again for hundreds of years. Peasant women were often partners in holding land, and they could inherit property. The work they did
in their homes and gardens was considered real work with
real value. They produced cloth and soap and medicine. Later,
as cities grew, women worked in hundreds of professions, as
smiths, butchers, bakers, ale brewers, and retailers. But then,
during the transition to capitalism, they lost the right to make
contracts and represent themselves in court. Not carrying a
baby to term became a crime punishable by death. And when
married women earned money, their wages were paid to their
husbands. Their work, unpaid and compulsory, was now to
produce more workers.

Witches were old women who could no longer produce children, midwives who facilitated birth control, childless women
who remained unproductive, loose women who refused to be

held as property, and prostitutes who sold themselves. Witches were, notably, poor. Among their recorded crimes were cursing the people who refused them food.

Women protested food shortages in the streets of seventeenth-century France and Spain. And women carried pitchforks and scythes in riots against English landowners. They tore down fences and dug up hedges at night. They set fields on fire to protest the enclosure of the commons as private property. While women participated in real rebellions—class rebellions—the witch hunts were fueled by an imagined conspiracy among women, in league with the devil. "The witch," Federici writes, "was the communist and terrorist of her time."

Women in medieval drawings and stories were headstrong, rough, and lusty. They rode men and lashed them with whips. They married five husbands, one after another, and would happily take a sixth. Women were insatiable and domineering, or so they appeared in the cartoons of that time. But after the witch hunts, on our side of history, women were drawn as meek and weak. And a new ideal woman emerged: "sexless, obedient, submissive, resigned to subordination." A woman, under capitalism, was no longer considered dangerous—she was helpless.

MOTHER'S HELPER

I'm counting out cash for the women I will pay this week, $40 for the Monday sitter and $60 for the Wednesday sitter. I became an employer when I became a mother—I was still weak from the blood loss of childbirth when I hired my first employee. She was a young woman, just out of high school, who came to my apartment two mornings a week. Mother's helper was her job title and she made $8 per hour. She held the baby while I did chores, or she did chores while I held the baby. The baby was always crying, held or not. And I was unwashed and unnerved. Mother's Helper turned a load of white laundry pink and I was not kind. She wasn't helping. But it seemed that I couldn't be helped. Despite my service to the baby, he was never satisfied. And I, in turn, was never satisfied with Mother's Helper. When she quit, I was relieved. But I had not yet gone back to teaching, or to writing.

"How any woman with a family ever put pen to paper I cannot fathom," Virginia Woolf wrote in 1930. Her cook was in the hospital, so Woolf couldn't write for two weeks. She was busy interviewing new cooks and washing greasy dishes. In the house where she grew up, eleven family members lived alongside seven servants. The servants cooked, scrubbed pans, polished silverware, cared for children, bought groceries, took deliveries, washed clothes, swept floors, beat rugs, laid fires, raked out ashes, emptied chamber pots, and heated water for their mistresses' baths.

"For century after century most women expected either to be servants or to keep servants," Alison Light writes in her book *Mrs. Woolf and the Servants.* And "giving or taking orders was the most common relationship between women." That remained true in England even through the 1930s, when unmarried women were looking for jobs as shopgirls or teachers instead of as servants.

Woolf wrote about her servants constantly, in her diary and her letters, but not with understanding. She recorded arguments and tears, threats and reconciliations. She tried to be "cordial." But the sound of them working bothered her. It was "detestable, hearing servants moving about." They talked too much and they were stupid. "The poor have no sense of humour," she complained. She was disgusted by their bad teeth, their big arms, and their sweat. Even paying them gave her a "feeling of waste." The work her servants performed was not considered labor, so their pay was not their wages but their keep. She kept other women and this made her uncomfortable. She wanted to be rid of them but she couldn't cook. And the work of running her household was a full-time job.

Woolf lived on income from property she had inherited, and some investments, until she began to earn money from her writing. "I'm one of those who are hampered by the psychological hindrance of owning capital," she noted in her diary. She argued to her friends that they should all surrender everything they had. Her husband, a socialist, thought this was nonsense. They should keep their property, he insisted, and do "good work."

Woolf learned to cook in her middle age, which freed her to fire the cook who had lived with her for eighteen years. But she kept a maid and a gardener who lived in cottages owned by her husband. The servants were no longer in her home, though still on her property. "The best servant," Light writes, "was a kind of absent presence."

Woolf dreamed of "an enchanted world where I turn a handle and hot mutton chops shoot out." I now live in that enchanted world, full of instant food and convenient machines—the hot water heater, the washing machine, the dishwasher, the flush toilet, the microwave, the stove that lights itself and doesn't need to be fed fuel.

"How many slaves work for you?" asks a website that will quantify the forced labor that produced my appliances, my clothes, my one gold ring, my leather shoes, my stereo, my phone, and my computer. Fifty is the answer. That includes the Uzbek children who picked the cotton for my clothes and the Congolese children who mined the tantalum for my electronics.

Servants cook for me, anonymously, in the kitchens of restaurants, and waitresses take my orders. But they don't share my property. And neither does the woman who comes to clean my floors every few months, or every month when there's money. I rarely see her and we talk only by text. She comes while I'm at work and takes the $160 I've left for her. When I return home, I find the things she recovered from behind the couch and under the bed—a creased book, a wine cork, the bathtub from Monopoly. These are laid out on the table like a museum exhibit.

JOAN DIDION

I think I see Joan Didion, improbably, behind the wheel of a minivan. She passes me on my bicycle and I catch a glimpse of her from behind. This has happened before. I've seen her waiting in line at the pharmacy, her face turned away, and then she's gone.

I once had a terrible argument about Didion with my mother. She picked up a book from my coffee table, read some of it, and then tossed it back down, saying, Crazy bitch. It occurred to me only later, after both of us were done crying, that what my mother found crazy about Didion was her wealth.

Her crimes are many, Didion. She's thin, she's cool, she's rich. She doesn't interrogate her privilege, though neither do the men of her moment—Norman Mailer, John McPhee, and Tom Wolfe in his white suit. I was primed for that argument with my mother, I was angry already, because I'd read a book review that suggested Didion neglected her child for her work.

I was just back to work after having a child and the crazy bitch, I was sure, was me.

There she is, Didion, on the verandah of the Royal Hawaiian Hotel in Honolulu, where she spends "an eccentric amount of time." This is a wink, an acknowledgment of her money and how she spends it. She works for her money, writing essays and articles and screenplays, but she also married into money and was born into economic security. That's where the Didion of "Slouching Towards Bethlehem" came from, the Didion who couldn't make sense of the hippies, and who didn't sympathize with the inarticulate impulse to just give up and drop out. The hippies, she thought, must be underinformed on the rules of the game—there is no dropping out.

The Diggers, who also appeared in that essay, were more-principled economic dropouts. Didion wanted to talk with them, but they didn't want to talk with her. They wrote and published for themselves, printing broadsides that critiqued the hippies. They were the counterculture to the counterculture. The Diggers would go on to provide free health care in the Haight-Ashbury and run a free bakery and stock free stores with things that had been discarded but were still good. Didion didn't mention, and perhaps didn't know, that they took their name from the Diggers of 1649, another small band of economic dissidents who wanted to build an egalitarian society. She found them somewhat ridiculous.

But that was Didion before *Salvador,* before *Miami,* before *Political Fictions*. Before most of her work. Before "New York: Sentimental Journeys," in which she concludes that the reason the rape of one white investment banker in Central Park captured more attention than any of the other 3,254 rapes reported in New York City in 1989 was that it seemed to be the story the city wanted to tell itself. That story, an upper-class fantasy, "was of a city systematically ruined, violated, raped by its underclass." It was a story, she observes, that reversed reality. The rich of the city wanted to believe that the poor made them unsafe, not the other way around.

"We tell ourselves stories in order to live" was printed triumphantly across a banner at a writing conference I once attended. Had they read the rest of that paragraph, I wondered. Because what she means is not that stories are the stuff of life, but that we lie to ourselves. Self-deception has always been her subject. And this is why she follows me in a minivan.

TEA

Robyn and I walk fifty blocks down Madison Avenue, which doesn't upset me as much as it used to. I'm not trying to live here now. We pass a shop window with one tiny purse on a pedestal flanked by two giant smiley-face balloons. The shops themselves, Robyn says, seem to understand that spending at this level can only be absurd.

She tells me about the exhibit she just saw at the Museum of Arts and Design, where gold kudzu with two thousand leaves wound around the entire gallery. At the Jewish Museum she watched a video of ants going about their work, carrying their food and their dead across a patch of grassy dirt that was, she later learned, Marx's grave.

We stop at the Morgan Library and order a lavish tea—tiny sandwiches and tiny scones and tiny loaves of bread with tiny pots of clotted cream, all served on a tiered silver tray. This building and the collection of art and artifacts within it once belonged to J. P. Morgan. In 1907 he locked his fellow bankers in here with his collection and refused to let them out until they agreed on a plan to rescue the economy. This was before the Federal Reserve was established and after Morgan had acquired the largest corporation in the world, a collection of mines, mills, and railroads called US Steel. Morgan financed the *Titanic*, but he didn't go down with it. He missed the boat. Now his name is on the bank that finances the credit card I use to pay for the tea.

The silver tray is a reminder that tea was once a luxury in England, before it became more common than beer. The queen and her court drank tea in the seventeenth century but in the eighteenth century it became a staple for wageworkers. It woke them up for work and replaced the meals they no longer had time to eat. Brewing tea was faster than baking bread or making broth, and a weak tea was cheap enough to have instead. The families of women who worked in mills had tea rather than porridge for breakfast. By the latter half of the nineteenth century, the diet of the poor would be composed mostly of white bread, tea, and sugar—all once luxuries of the rich. The tea was grown on British-owned plantations in India and sweetened with sugar from plantations worked by slaves in the Caribbean. Tea was a poor substitute for food, but it was warm and sweet, a comfort and a pleasure. It was an everyday luxury afforded to workers by the deprivations of other workers. And it's the colonial legacy we're still drinking.

We're not here for tea, but for the exhibit of Emily Dickinson's letters and manuscripts. I study a photograph of students making donuts at Mount Holyoke Female Seminary, which she attended for a year. She dropped out and is not in the photo. I examine a drawing she sent to a friend of a plant from her garden and a poem she wrote on the flap of an envelope. She often wrote on little scraps of paper, I hear a museum guide say. Paper was expensive. An entire book has been made of the poems that she wrote on the backs of envelopes. I inspect one of the ten poems that were published in her lifetime, anonymously, as her name never appeared in print. Dickinson wasn't eager for her work to be published, the guide explains. Her father disapproved of women writing, but she may have had other reasons. I think of the line from "I'm Nobody! Who are you?" that Dickinson changed. *Don't tell! they'd banish us – you know!* became *Don't tell! they'd advertise – you know!*

She didn't want to be advertised, she just wanted to do her work, her writing. Her other work was caring for her mother, who was ill, and baking for her father, who would eat only bread made by her hand. She held a job briefly, when she was a student, cleaning knives.

MINE

I'm trying to memorize a poem by Emily Dickinson. I already have one stanza, I think, but then I begin to recite it and I have only the first two lines: *I am afraid to own a Body – / I am afraid to own a Soul –*

Once I have it, Josh tells me, it will be hard to give away. Nobody will want it. He has hundreds of poems memorized—"The World Is Too Much with Us" and "The Bean Eaters" and "The Emperor of Ice Cream." The only person he can recite them to, he says, is his wife. He carries a laminated pamphlet in his breast pocket, folded into thirds, a list of all the poems he knows. Standing on the train platform, or waiting in line at the grocery store, he takes out this list and recites a poem in his mind. If he doesn't practice them, he loses them.

I'm intrigued by his collection, so precarious, requiring constant maintenance, and worth nothing. It produces no appreciation in value, just practice.

I've mastered the first stanza now but I don't have the second stanza because I keep forgetting the phrase "entailed at pleasure," a play on the legal language of property. Dickinson's father was an attorney, concerned with property, his own and others'. When she was twenty-five, her father bought back the family homestead that his father had mortgaged and lost to debt. That was in 1855, the year Massachusetts passed its married women's property act, giving women the right to own and sell property. Under the law of coverture that preceded this act, a married woman could not own property as she herself was property, legally one with her husband.

Possession was among Dickinson's preoccupations. In one poem, she uses the word *mine* six times in nine lines, claiming something unnamed:

> Mine – by the Right of the White Election!
> Mine – by the Royal Seal!
> Mine – by the sign in the Scarlet prison –
> Bars – cannot conceal!
>
> Mine – here – in Vision – and in Veto!
> Mine – by the Grave's Repeal –
> Titled – Confirmed –
> Delirious Charter!
> Mine – long as Ages steal!

What is it, scholars wonder, that she's made hers by election, veto, repeal, and charter, entirely outside the law? She's writing as Hester Prynne from *The Scarlet Letter*, Elizabeth Phillips suggests, and giving Hester the last word denied by Hawthorne, claiming her independence. Maybe she's Hester, I think, and maybe she's also herself. Maybe what she's claiming, giddily, is her own disobedience. Her refusal to be saved, to marry, to leave her room to see visitors. Maybe she's claiming her own poetry, her work. Or maybe she's not claiming anything at all—maybe she's going in drag, dressing up in the sensation of ownership, the mindset of possession, the thrill of illicit entitlement.

Dickinson never owned any property herself. She died in her father's house, the house he willed to her brother. And her garden was worked by a man her father hired to dig for her. *I had some things that I called mine*, she wrote of the garden, *And God, that he called his*. The garden was hers until frost killed the plants in the fall, when her domain was reclaimed. The lesson being, James Guthrie writes, "that ownership of all kinds is a precarious business at best, or at worst, a form of self-delusion."

WORK

Ray is thinking of selling his restaurant, John says. When Ray first quit his job and started to cook, John helped him refinish tabletops. Soon there was a line of people outside his restaurant. We had breakfast with Ray at Ina's and the Breakfast Queen of Chicago herself came out of the kitchen to ask him if he liked her French toast. That happens everywhere he goes, John says, chefs come out to shake his hand. Ray lives in a new house now and drives a new car. But he still works seventy hours a week and his job doesn't provide health insurance.

Ray invited us to invest some money in the restaurant back before it opened. But we were saving our money for a house. Barbecue, traditional food of the poor, doesn't have much of a margin. Big slabs of meat have to be smoked for fifteen hours at a time. The supply costs and the labor costs are both high, John notes. I yawn and he asks if I think this is boring and I say that I just find it exhausting, the calculus of wringing profit out of other people's work.

John is irritated with me now. He says I'm using the language of Marx to talk about real lives. I'm using the only language I know, and there are real lives behind the term *labor costs*, too. Ray just wants to live like us, John says. And now I understand why he's mad. He thinks that I think we deserve more time off and better benefits than Ray does. But I don't see much evidence that what anyone gets for their work has anything to do with what they deserve.

You and I, John says, are essentially making barbecue for the university. What we do isn't any different from what Ray does. But it is, I say. Our work doesn't produce a pulled pork sandwich—we don't make a product. And we're not entrepreneurs—we occupy two desks in the basement of a large bureaucracy. We don't sign anyone's paycheck or tell anyone they can't work more hours. We don't feel compelled, as Ray does, to lend our employees money when they can't make rent. We get to pretend that nobody else is paid less for their time so that we can be paid more. And when we're in the classroom we can imagine ourselves as our own bosses, bosses without employees.

ART

I'm teaching a night class and most of my students work during the day. They are public school teachers and corporate consultants and parents who write at night. One of them composes music. While I sit in the empty classroom waiting for the students to arrive, I read the essay the composer has written for today's class.

It begins with him arriving in a practice room with a thermos of coffee and sitting down at the piano. First, he asks himself what feeling he wants to convey and what relationship his music should have to the great music of the past. The question of the past is bottomless, so he retreats. He's back now to the question of what this music should feel like. Paradise, he decides, but he doesn't know what paradise feels like. Does this feeling need a new melody, different from the ten measures he wrote yesterday? Yes, he decides. But how many sections should the melody have? At this point, he needs to go to the bathroom. On return, he's aggravated to find that the notes he jotted down before he left have not progressed in his absence. The music has not become better without him. He needs to answer some questions about how this melody will relate to the melody he has already written. He puts down some notes, changes one, then changes the rhythm and changes it back. He takes the fragment he has written and repeats it, with some minor variations. He's getting somewhere now! But where is this going? And what is the point of all this? He feels defeated, so he leaves the practice room where he has been all day, having written two measures, a few seconds of music.

Class still hasn't started but some students are here. My clothes are damp because it began to rain as I rode my bicycle to this old mansion by the lake. While I open the windows to warm the overcooled room, letting in the humid air coming off the lake, I talk with the composer about his essay. I tell him that it precisely captured my moment-to-moment experience of writing—the unending interrogation, the missteps, the slowness, the frustration. He and I are talking about the agonies of our work now while another student listens.

If that's how it makes you feel, she says, then why do you do it? Because there's no other choice, I'm tempted to answer, if you're compelled to make art. But I think she's asking where the pleasure is in this work. It's in the making, I know that much, though the process itself isn't exactly pleasurable. It is, as the composer chronicled, a series of difficult questions. Attending to those questions demands both work and labor.

Maybe I need another word. Casting about, I come up with *service*. We're in service to the art, I tell my student, bent to it. There's pleasure in this posture, in being bettered by the work. It isn't the pleasure of mastery, but the pleasure of being mastered.

MASTERED

Service doesn't mean exactly what I thought it did. I'm paging through meaning after meaning, noun and verb, in three different dictionaries. "Willing bondage" is how Lewis Hyde describes the service of the artist who is working to master an art, but *art* doesn't appear in these definitions. Service is the act of paying interest on a debt, labor that doesn't produce a commodity, and a ceremony of religious worship. That's something close to what I had in mind.

Service was a way of life in Northern Europe in the Middle Ages, David Graeber writes. Almost everyone was expected to spend some part of their early lives, seven to fifteen years, as a servant. Older children and teenagers, boys and girls both, were sent by their parents to work as servants in other households. This was true even for the elite, who would serve as pages or ladies-in-waiting before becoming knights and noblewomen. This period of service, an extended adolescence, was training for adulthood. A manner of living or a craft or a trade was learned through service. It was an education. Ideally, the servant emerged from service mature and disciplined, ready to start her own household. And then the servant became the master, in turn, to servants.

Service is "the condition of our being," Virginia Woolf's mother wrote centuries later, in defense of the Victorian institution of service. We don't choose service, she suggested, we are born to it. "Service was not simply a throwback to a pre-industrial past," Alison Light notes, it was an ethic, informed by the Christian ideal of selfless giving. "Generations of men found their self-esteem in the idea of serving their country at home or abroad, being a 'public servant' in the new Civil 'Service,' in the colonial 'service,' as a 'servant' of a bank, or a government 'servant,' or in the 'services.'"

It was a calling, a duty. Service was a contribution to society, heroic even. But in the home, service was care and maintenance. It was nursing the sick. It was tending to the baby. Service involved feces and food and dishwater. It was done out of love and duty and desperation. At its best, it was intensely intimate. "Service could be brutalizing and estranging," Light writes, "it could also be affectionate and devoted, but, however unequal the parties, it was always something more, or less, than a purely financial arrangement."

Service, in the Victorian era, was a relationship of mutual obligation. Unequal, but mutual. Woolf's mother compared it to friendship, or the relationship between a mother and a child.

Virginia didn't see it that way. She would not pretend to be a friend or mother to her servants. The old ways of thinking about service were falling away in her time. "Stripped bare of the flummery, the fine words and good intentions, all that remained was the nakedness of caste feeling, the dog beneath the skin," Light writes. Virginia hated it, the service relationship. And she longed to be free of all obligations to other people. But that sort of freedom can only be found at the bottom of the Ouse.

During her recovery from an overdose of sleeping medication, one of Virginia's therapies was cleaning the drawing room. Years later, shortly before she drowned herself, she began scrubbing the floors of her house on her hands and knees. It was a desperate bid to remain alive. Her doctor had advised her to keep busy, and noted privately that it would do her good to "harrow a field." She spent hours beating the carpets and then watched the dust from the carpets settle onto the books she had just dusted. The day she died, she worked alongside her maid all morning. Then she put down her duster and walked into the river.

WORK

John, just home from work, asks how my day was and I say that it was okay but that I didn't do any of my work because I was busy doing housework. Whose work is that? he asks slyly. If it isn't mine, it might be his.

I've just read an article in the *New York Times* about a white composer who has reached new heights of productivity since entering into a dominant-submissive relationship with a black woman. He's the dominant partner, according to the *Times*, but his domination is not primarily sexual. His wife, who finds submission satisfying, attends to all his needs while he works at composing for fourteen hours a day.

At first, I don't understand why it's news that a man who has a woman doing all his housework is finding himself productive. But then I think maybe this is progress. Maybe what's news is that now we're calling this domination, when we used to just call it marriage.

Jenny Marx was picking up Karl's cigar butts and keeping track of his spending even before they were married. Later, she served as his secretary and fended off creditors and bore one child after another while he wrote *Capital*. Jenny was one of the only people who could read his handwriting, so she prepared his manuscripts for publishers. She copied *The Communist Manifesto* in her own hand, and then she mentioned in a letter that she was overwhelmed with housework. A hundred years later, the artist Mierle Laderman Ukeles would ask, "After the revolution, who's going to pick up the garbage on Monday morning?"

John has never cleaned a toilet in our house, of this I'm fairly certain. But I never take out the garbage. We both wash dishes. The floors are an unclaimed territory, a no-man's-land. Neither of us cleans them for months at a time. We pay a Polish woman to sweep and mop for us. Mollie doesn't think this is a good solution. Paying another woman is just outsourcing the oppression, she tells me. She seems to be suggesting that the only ethical way to deal with housework is for all of us to clean up after ourselves. Or live in our own messes.

If you pay well and tip generously, Daryl argues, what's wrong with having someone else do the work? Isn't housecleaning, she asks, just like any other work? It seems not to be. The phrase *cleaning toilets* is shorthand for demeaning work. Daryl and I are talking about this because our friend the immigration lawyer, who works fourteen-hour days, wants to hire a cleaning woman but her husband the public defender is against it on principle.

Well then, cleaning their house should be his job, I suggest. But if a woman is going to do housecleaning, isn't it better for her to be paid than for her to do it for free? I rethink this line of argument almost as soon as I speak it. I could also say that prostitution is better than everyday sex, in that a woman is getting paid for something that many women do for free. When it's good, sex is more pleasurable than housework, but being paid for it doesn't necessarily make it better. It just makes it work.

Marx very probably impregnated his maid, Helene Demuth. Helene had worked for Jenny's mother since she was eleven, and was sent to live with Karl and Jenny when she was twenty-five, shortly after they married. She worked for them until they died, and when she died she was buried with them. She had no family of her own, as her baby was given to a foster family and the pregnancy was blamed on Engels.

I'm sick of cleaning up for her, John jokes as we pick up stacks of paper and piles of laundry to ready our house for the woman who cleans the floors. This woman, who doesn't speak English well, is trying to put a child through college. That's all I know about her. I don't know if she wants her work to be cleaning and I don't know if she feels like she has a choice.

The composer's wife has a choice, this much I know. Her situation is feminist, she tells the *Times*, because she has chosen it freely, for her own pleasure.

I wonder if she thinks of what she is doing as work. She calls it service.

SERVICE

"I find intense fulfillment in being able to serve in this way," the composer's wife says. And yes, she's aware of how it looks— a direct descendent of chattel slaves serving a white man. But her service is entirely consensual, not forced. And she won't be told that she can't play out her own personal psychodrama, she says, just because she's black.

Her name is Mollena Williams-Haas. Her pet name for her husband, who is Austrian, is Herr Meister. Mister Master. I find this funny, but I still pause the YouTube video of her delivering a talk at a sexuality conference when she calls her husband her "owner" and herself his "slave."

In the video she appears with her husband, a mousy man. She does all the talking at first, and when her husband begins to speak she adjusts the way he holds his microphone. She interrupts him. She corrects his imperfect English, clarifies what he means, and makes jokes at his expense.

As if she knows what I'm thinking, she begins to recount a story about being told repeatedly that she wasn't very "slave-like." Having just accepted her own desire to be a slave, she found this painful. She was told that if she wanted to be a slave, she had to be quiet and she had to be invisible. She should not call attention to herself and she should not stand out. Hearing this, she thought, "I guess I'm not a slave." But then she met a woman who told her, "If your heart draws you to slavery and to service, go to it. Don't let anybody tell you what slavery means."

Maybe her true fetish is irony, Lisa says. We're drinking wine on Lisa's porch and laughing about this inspirational speech devoted to owning your own slavery, but I'm seriously inspired. She just wants to be a slave on her own terms, I say. That's a kind of liberation. "There are people who love rope bondage who will instruct, knot by knot, the person who is tying them up, exactly how they want to be tied up," Williams-Haas says. And that's all I want out of my work—to be tied up the way I want to be tied up.

Lisa is an artist, and her day job, which is also her night job, is caring for her three children while her wife, a banker, works. The terms of her service are not stipulated in any contract. Even before she was married, Williams-Haas had a contract with her husband that guaranteed her, among other things, health care coverage. Her contract also improved upon the standard marriage contract by including a guiding principle drawn from BDSM: "It is the primary responsibility of the slave to protect the master's property at all times, up to and including protecting the property from the master."

Property and *owner* are the words Williams-Haas sometimes prefers over *slave* and *master.* Not all of her power play is race play, but she understands that it can look that way. She is always bound, in other people's minds, to performing her race. "Racism and bigotry and the pain they engender are real," she writes. "But how often do we have the ironic opportunity to consent to and control our own pain? I have discovered that consenting to small amounts of pain and abuse and suffering is like an inoculation of my soul against the pandemic of hatred."

My Google search for "race play" produces an article that profiles a Latino man who got into sex work because a clinic in his city was offering free health care for sex workers. He was a young artist and he didn't have health insurance. He discovered, doing sex work, that some men wanted to use his body to play out racist fantasies. Before he became a sex worker, he felt wounded when a lover used racial slurs during sex. But it was easier for him to accept this language at work, in a "commodified exchange," which was a kind of drag, he says, because "it was something that I could put on and take off." He considered it a service to allow other men to exorcise their racist impulses on him.

Williams-Haas's slavery might be play, but her service is real. And service, she maintains, can be erotic even when it has nothing to do with sex. "The sensations I experienced in the face of learning to properly serve formal high tea," she writes, "felt a great deal to me like arousal." And here is where I begin to wonder if my preference for work that feels like service, and my gravitation to unpaid labor, is itself a kind of kink. Or power play, maybe. I, too, find service satisfying. And satisfaction, as Williams-Haas notes, can be hard to come by.

SATISFACTION

I'm drenched in cream, marinated in wine, basted in cognac, and thoroughly buttered by the end of *The Alice B. Toklas Cook Book*. I'm fascinated and horrified by the Omelette Aurore, eight eggs folded over candied fruits and chestnuts soaked for several hours in curaçao liqueur, with frangipani cream poured on top, all of this then sprinkled with diced angelica, six powdered macaroons, and three tablespoons melted butter. These recipes call for liqueurs I've never tasted, herbs I don't know, meats I can't procure, and more time than I can spare. A hare must be pickled in vinegar and peppercorns for a day before it is browned and then cooked slowly for up to four hours, twenty-four figs must marinate in an excellent dry port wine for thirty-six hours before the wine is used to baste a roasting duck every fifteen minutes for an hour, a pound of chopped veal knuckle and a calf's foot must simmer with onion and carrot for four hours before their juice is put through a sieve and the sauce is thickened and then a chicken is browned while a bouillon is prepared from giblets cooked for over two hours. I believe her when she writes, "the sauce justifies the time spent," but I don't believe I can spend the time. Not until the last chapter, when she writes about gardening.

"There is nothing that is comparable to it, as satisfactory or as thrilling, as gathering the vegetables one has grown," Toklas writes. Tending the garden at the summer home she shared with Gertrude Stein was time consuming, even with help. A local boy did the heavy work while she watered and weeded and removed potato beetles by hand. She would spend an hour gathering tiny strawberries for Gertrude's breakfast. And a long time picking very young green beans for eight to ten people. Every fall, Alice filled basket after basket with carrots, pumpkins, squash, and eggplants. All this was shipped five hundred miles back to the apartment in Paris, at expense. "Looking at that harvest as an economic question, it was disastrous, but from the point of view of the satisfaction which work and aesthetic confer, it was sublime."

"She was an artist," Alice writes of a cook who carved a chicken at her table, assessing her own work with pride and pleasure. Fresh asparagus tips, bound in bundles and cooked in salted water, dressed in melted butter, and served with whipped cream were "a thing of beauty." As were her raspberries, hanging in red clusters from the bushes she had trellised and pruned. The care they required, she writes, was more of a pleasure than a labor.

When Gertrude asked Alice what she saw when she closed her eyes, she replied, "Weeds." The weeds were an endless torment. And when the war came, with rationing and a scarcity of meat, there was the unpleasant task of killing her own food. She writes with some despair of receiving an unexpected gift: "Six white pigeons to be smothered, to be plucked, to be cleaned and all this to be accomplished before Gertrude Stein returned, for she didn't like to see work being done."

Gertrude didn't like to do work, either, and mostly she didn't have to. Money from her family's real estate holdings and the sale of some paintings she had bought with that money afforded her the luxury of working solely on her writing. She was said to have had a talent for getting other people to do things for her, paid or unpaid. During the occupation, when food was scarce, Gertrude would sometimes return from her daily walk carrying eggs or butter. "It is not with money that one buys on the black market," Alice observed, "but with one's personality."

Gertrude had some fun with a photographer who wanted to take pictures of her doing everyday tasks like packing a suitcase or talking on the telephone. She couldn't do those things, she told the photographer, because Miss Toklas packed her suitcase and Miss Toklas handled her calls. Miss Toklas also typed her manuscripts. Finally, the photographer asked her what she could do, and she told him she could remove her own hat and drink a glass of water.

"It takes a lot of time to be a genius," Gertrude wrote, "you have to sit around so much doing nothing, really doing nothing."

Servants helped. There was beloved Frederich, who ran away in the night with a woman; Célestine, who was a terrible cook; Maria, who was a treasure; Hélène, highly capable in every way; Jeanne, who was scrupulously clean and attentive; Léonie, who cooked more than she cleaned; another Jeanne, this one mysterious and given to sudden disappearances; an unnamed Austrian woman who left after three days, dismayed that these Americans "lived French"; Margot, who tossed crêpes high in the air and lighted desserts aflame as she carried them into the dining room; Trac, who was restless and wanted his own restaurant; Nguyen, who had a drinking problem; Margit, who was melancholy and liked to read; and the indispensable Widow Roux, who washed and ironed and gave gardening advice. Alongside all of them, Alice cooked.

She was not a servant, Alice made clear. When she opened the door to a visitor who handed her flowers for Gertrude, as he would with a servant, Alice called out, "Look, Lovey, what Donald has brought me!" She was a manager, a secretary, a cook, a companion, a lover—a wife of her time and class. And she enjoyed it, lunching with friends on filet of sole, driving with Gertrude to Marseilles for bouillabaisse, cooking bass for Picasso, taking an ocean liner to America, getting two enormous crabs at Fisherman's Wharf in San Francisco, and tasting passion fruit for the first time.

When it was over, when Gertrude died, Alice was left with another twenty years and Gertrude's art collection. There were many Picassos in the collection, bought with Gertrude's trust money when Picasso was not yet famous, nearly stolen by Nazis during the occupation but saved, and now worth millions of dollars.

The art was hers, but not entirely hers—Gertrude had willed it to Alice for "use for life," and then it would go to Gertrude's relatives. This, along with having been a wife who was not legally a wife, caused Alice some difficulty. She wrote her cookbook in part because she needed money. Gertrude's relatives took the art off Alice's walls and stored it in a bank vault until she died, leaving blank outlines where the paintings had been. She didn't see the blanks, Alice wrote to a friend, she still saw the paintings. She was evicted from her apartment three years before she died. In the end, her name was engraved on the back of Gertrude's headstone, after a lifetime of Boeuf Bourguignon and Green Peas à la Good Wife.

TOIL

It's easier and harder, Mollie says. She means our work, the work of writing, compared to other work. We're walking along the lakefront downtown, with glass office buildings reflecting the sky on one side and white waves rolling in on the other. The sky is everywhere and there's water in the wind. What's harder about our work, she says, is that we can't walk away from it at the end of the day. It's always with us. We can't clock out.

Back in New York, when I left my job at the parks department for the day I was entirely done. And I left early because I started early. I would hurry through my paperwork in the morning to get to the other part of the job, walking the streets of the city inspecting community gardens and delivering shipments of dirt, which I shoveled from the back of a pickup truck. I shared an office with a Jamaican man who finally said, softly, You don't have to work so fast, you know. Office work, for him, was a reprieve from work in the field, as we called it. The field was five hundred gardens in all five boroughs of the city. Work in the field was never done, it was endless. He was pacing himself. And I was making him look bad, arriving early to file reports so that I could leave the air-conditioned office and walk around outside in the heat, where I wanted to be. He knew I wouldn't last long—I'd find an office job—and he would remain, working the field. He didn't have a college degree and he wasn't going to get another job. This, he explained to me, was his life.

Toil is the word Galbraith uses for work that is fatiguing and monotonous and a source of no particular pleasure. Like many people whose preferred work is not physical, he assumes most toil to be physical labor. In the 1998 edition of his 1958 book, he writes optimistically about "the continuing revolution in job quality being wrought by the computer," but he does not mention the toil introduced by the computer. The endless filling of little boxes, the esoteric software systems, the repetitive stress, the physical toll of sitting all day staring at a screen. And he does not foresee the unique drudgery of email, the electronic demands spilling out of the workday. In France, a law now requires large companies not to expect their employees to send or respond to emails after work hours. The "right to disconnect" it's called, an effort to reclaim the limits on a workweek hard won by labor protests of the past.

Mollie works more hours than I do and teaches more classes at a struggling university. She's a historian, doing research for the book she's writing when she isn't teaching. She doesn't know how much longer she'll have a job, because her university may cease to exist. Already, there is no longer a department of history.

"You're lucky to have a job," my adviser from graduate school told me when I asked him how to negotiate the terms of the teaching position I had just been offered, the one I still hold. Shortly before I graduated he told me drunkenly that he was a little bit in love with me, his first direct statement of attraction after years of uncomfortable innuendo. I needed his signature on my degree, so I ignored his guarded passes, not knowing what else to do. I had read that women did not negotiate as successfully as men and I wanted a man's advice on this. His advice—to the woman he loved a little bit—was not to ask for anything.

Out in the field, on a South Texas farm, a Mexican woman is working without gloves, picking cilantro for $3 a box, which will earn her $39 for a day of work from 5:00 a.m. to 6:00 p.m. I read about her in the newspaper as I lay in bed. The woman's mother, who was a paramedic in Mexico, now also works as a picker. She tells the reporter that she sees the supervisors leading young women to far corners of the field. She knows her rights as a worker, but she knows, too, that if she makes a complaint she could be deported.

WORK

I know why people hate Mexicans, John announces—they work harder than we do. He's just been outside talking with the men who are rebuilding our chimney. Last month, a royalty check for my most recent book arrived, money we didn't expect, so now we're spending it on the house, on the luxury of a fire in the fireplace. Really we're burning money.

John and I are both finding it difficult to write with this work going on. It's loud, but that's not the problem. From where I sit at my desk in the attic, I can see a man pushing a load of bricks in a wheelbarrow up a ramp. I watch him from behind my computer screen as he slowly heaves the load into the bed of a truck.

"A lurking sense of guilt over a more pleasant, agreeable and remunerative life can often be assuaged," Galbraith writes, "by the observation, 'I am a worker too,' or, more audaciously, by the statement that 'mental labor is far more taxing than physical labor.'" The conviction that mental labor and physical labor are at least equivalent, he notes, was one thing Cold War capitalists and communists had in common. The president of a corporation and his employee on the assembly line and the communist official and his comrade on a collective farm all called what they did by the same name: work.

How much of the $13,000 that we're paying to have our chimney rebuilt, I ask John, is going to the men who are doing the work? About half, he guesses. He worked construction once, at $7 an hour. He considers the factors—there are five men on the job, some highly skilled, climbing up and down a scaffold in the heat for eight days. Yes, he decides, about half. The owner of the chimney repair company mentioned that these masons have been working for him for eighteen years. Some of them might even have health insurance.

When the Service Employees International Union began organizing the untenured teachers on our campus, one of my colleagues complained that it was the wrong union for us. I wondered if he objected to the idea that our work is service. We don't belong in the same union, he argued, as nurses and janitors. But if the strength of a union is in numbers, I thought, then it wouldn't hurt the nurses and janitors to be joined by teachers.

The vote to unionize—which was won by a narrow margin, contested by the university, and then overturned in court— probably wouldn't have increased his pay or mine. We make too much already. The people it would have helped most are the teachers who are paid by the class, as adjuncts. Both he and I hold the highest rank available to the lowest-ranking faculty, meaning that we're at the top of the bottom. Or the bottom of the top, if we consider the office staff and the computer technicians and the food-service workers and the unseen cleaners who vacuum the rugs and empty the trash cans in our offices at night. We're the upper-middle class of the university. And so we can, in our minds, align ourselves with the tenured professors and the deans at the top. But that serves them, I think, more than it serves anyone else.

The idea that unions are for people in bad jobs and that people in good jobs don't need to negotiate the terms of their service depends on the belief that good jobs are inherently good and can't be made bad, or more menial. It's a white-collar fantasy. "The blue-collar blues is no more bitterly sung than the white-collar moan," Studs Terkel writes in *Working*. "'I'm a machine,' says the spot-welder. 'I'm caged,' says the bank teller, and echoes the hotel clerk. 'I'm a mule,' says the steelworker. 'A monkey can do what I do,' says the reception-ist. 'I'm less than a farm implement,' says the migrant worker. 'I'm an object,' says the high-fashion model. Blue collar and white call upon the identical phrase: 'I'm a robot.'"

Roughly a third of all jobs, David Graeber estimates, are what he calls "bullshit jobs." These jobs are so pointless that even the people doing the jobs don't see any reason for them to exist. Bullshit jobs aren't shit jobs, the distinction being that shit jobs involve essential work that needs to be done—what makes them shit is that the workers who do these jobs are badly treated, undervalued, and poorly paid. "Shit jobs tend to be blue collar and pay by the hour," Graeber observes, "whereas bullshit jobs tend to be white collar and salaried." Bullshit jobs are not usually dangerous or physically demanding. And they pay well. But they don't offer any of the rewards of service or the satisfaction of having done something worthwhile. Many of them involve doing nothing at all. Where shit jobs often expose a worker's body to harm, bullshit jobs cause psychological harm.

"Daily meaning as well as daily bread," Terkel writes, is what people are looking for in work, "a sort of life rather than a Monday through Friday sort of dying." Among the people Terkel interviews, the farmer and the flight attendant and the prostitute and the stockbroker, there are some who take deep pleasure in their work—the stonemason, the piano tuner, the bookbinder, the carpenter who is also a poet. The janitor doesn't mind being a janitor. He doesn't want to be called a building engineer. "You can call me a janitor," he says. "There's nothing wrong with a janitor." But he does mind the pain in his back when he shovels snow and when he uses a mop.

A study of job satisfaction among hospital janitors found that the janitors who reported the greatest satisfaction were the ones who thought of their work as caring for the sick, though their job description was a list of duties like "collect and dispose of soiled linens" and "stock restroom supplies." When these janitors described their work, they talked of visiting the patients who had the least visitors, joking with patients to cheer them up, writing letters to patients who had gone home and might be lonely, and carefully cleaning the rooms of the patients who were most vulnerable to infection. Without changing jobs, without joining a union, the janitors improved their work life by caring for people. Part of what makes a job good, they understood, is the sense that what you do matters.

When the head mason comes to the door to tell me that the job is done, I say that I've already been outside to look at the finished chimney and I've seen that sometime in the far future when we're all gone and this house has fallen down, that chimney will still be standing. I'm thinking of the lone chimney in the rocky woods where I grew up, the chimney that long outlived its maker. The mason smiles and shakes his head, laying a hand affectionately on the brickwork of our house. This house isn't going to fall down, he says, this is good work.

PLAY

That's not your work, the mother sitting next to me at the playground says to her son, who has taken a toy from another child. In Montessori school, she tells me, play is called work. I've heard this before and it bothers me.

Let play be play, I think. It's not work. But then I begin to wonder what makes play different from work. Is it that play, like art, is unpaid and impractical? Play is sport and theater, movement, touch. There's foreplay, swordplay, and wordplay. *Play* has dozens of definitions. *Free* and *freedom* appear in many of them. But so does *work*. And then there's Fred Rogers, who says: "For children play is serious learning. Play is the real work of childhood."

The city wants to tear down this playground, which was built twenty-five years ago by a group of neighbors who cleared away trash from a vacant lot and hammered the wooden planks together themselves. Our alderman has announced that it will be replaced with a new playground made of plastic. It's time to upgrade, he says. This playground is like an outdated cell phone.

At the next city council meeting, Alex, who runs a bike shop down the street where he salvages old bicycles, lists all the ways in which the playground is not like a cell phone. But the alderman has a new argument now—the problem is not that the playground is old, the problem is that it's unsafe.

Safety, or litigation really, is what razed the playgrounds of my childhood. But statistics reveal that just as many children get injured on playgrounds now as they did back then. Safer playgrounds aren't actually safer. John made fires in the alley as a child, unsupervised. That's the white trash philosophy of play, he says. It's also the philosophy of the Norwegian early-childhood education expert who maintains that fire is an essential component of productive play, along with heights, sharp tools, fighting, and solitude. There are dissertations devoted to why children need this kind of play, and psychologists warning us to save play from safety.

The playground inspector hired by the city confirms in his official report that the playground needs repairs, but he doesn't recommend tearing it down. This playground, he says, is like a 1965 Mustang. If you have a classic car that doesn't run, you can rebuild the engine and restore it to its original condition, but you can't replace it with a new car. No new cars are like the 1965 Mustang, he says. And play, I think, isn't what it used to be.

ART

You have to be appointed before you can be disappointed, Robyn says. True, I laugh. Her wordplay is a revelation, play that does real work.

Now I'm alone on Robyn's back porch, looking out at the tall grasses of her yard. Robyn doesn't garden, she ungardens, as she puts it. In the August humidity, I feel a rising euphoria. I recognize this as the aura that precedes the work of writing, like the aura that precedes a seizure or a migraine. An idea is hovering before me, spectral and electric. The idea is just slightly out of reach and I will spend hours at my desk before I can grasp it, before I can work it on the page. But it is here now in the weeds, ungardened.

Robyn returns with a stack of poetry, June Jordan and Wanda Coleman and Robert Frost. My words, *work* and *play*, sent her to search her shelves for work and play. She opens *The Complete Poems of Robert Frost* to "Two Tramps in Mud Time" and reads aloud.

Frost was splitting logs in his yard when two men walked out of the woods, lumberjacks looking for work. "Hit them hard!" one man yelled, and Frost knew what he was saying. The man wanted Frost to hire him to split those logs. But it was early spring, a thaw, and Frost wanted to do the job himself. He loved the work, the weight of the ax in his hands and the pull of the earth at his feet. *The life of muscles rocking soft / And smooth and moist in vernal heat.*

The pleasure of splitting a log, I know, is not unlike the pleasure of hitting the right sentence, a sentence that splits open to reveal a meaning that was, just moments ago, trapped in wood. As a teenager I split logs for my mother, for the woodstove that heated her house. I listen now to Robyn's voice, so sure in handling the heft of a line, and I can feel the momentum of the falling ax. In my hands, the ax would often bounce off the log, leaving hardly a dent. Or, with luck, it would leave a crack into which I could insert an iron wedge. And then I would swing the blunt end of the ax at that wedge. Mostly I would miss, and the log would tumble over. But sometimes I would hit it dead-on, powerfully, and the log would fall cleanly in two, the scent of sap released. Then I would stand there in astonishment, my ears stinging from the ring of iron on iron, the red center of the wood steaming before me, a revelation.

He had no right to play, Frost thought, with work that other men did for pay. Or if he did, his right was love. Their right was need. *Theirs was the better right—agreed.* But still, he wouldn't separate the two. *Only where love and need are one, / And the work is play for mortal stakes, / Is the deed ever really done / For Heaven and the future's sakes.*

Yes, I think, my work is play—play for mortal stakes.

THE GAME

I'm about to load the dishwasher when John says, Load that dishwasher. I ignore him and pick up a sponge to clean the counter. We're gonna want that counter cleaned too, he says. I turn around. He's holding a dustpan and a broom. Let's see some sweeping over there, I say. He smirks as he bends down to sweep up the coffee grounds around the trash can. I'm leaning against the counter now, laughing. He says, If you can lean, you can clean.

The name of this game is Assistant Manager. And the fun of it is that it's maddening. I couldn't play it at first because my irritation over being told what to do would flare into real anger and then John would laugh at my anger, making me angrier. John has been playing this game since high school, when he worked at the grocery store where he learned Assistant Manager.

J wants to know what we're laughing about, so I explain the game. If you're the employee, which it's better not to be, the goal is to maintain your composure when the assistant manager tells you what to do. If you can, you should find a way to manage the assistant manager—try to make the assistant manager work for you. If you're the assistant manager, who always initiates the game, the goal is to act like you're in charge and tell someone to do something they were already going to do, as if it was your idea, so they'll feel like they're taking orders.

Mama, he says, you do that to me all the time and you're not even playing. I pause. Yes, that's true, though I don't want it to be. And this isn't a game—it's practice for work.

INVESTMENT

WORK

My work today consists of listening to a man I call The Vest talk. He's been talking for thirty-five minutes, the entirety of this meeting, with six women sitting around the table listening to him. He speaks slowly, deliberately, softly, using the cadences of someone who is unfolding a story. He allows himself ample preamble and endless asides, but he says nothing. Listening to him reminds me of driving across the Midwest— all those changeless hours in which you sense the momentum of the car but still feel like you aren't going anywhere, just through more corn.

While he talks, I'm thinking about manners. "A symbolic pantomime of mastery on the one hand and of subservience on the other," Veblen writes of manners. The *man* in the word *manners* is the *man* that means hand, Robyn wrote to me in one of her letters about manners. And a gentleman used to be a man who did not work with his hands, I wrote back. Charles Mann marvels that so many British colonists could have starved at Chesapeake Bay, where the waters were rich with fish. The problem, he suggests, was that too high a proportion of the colonists defined themselves as gentlemen, and thus could not fish.

We have something to discuss at this meeting that The Vest would prefer to avoid. I look down to the head of the table, at the woman who's running the meeting. Her face is flushed with frustration, but she isn't going to say anything. She's impeccably polite, like everyone here. I want to send her a telegram: HE IS USING OUR MANNERS AGAINST US STOP. She looks away.

Later, too late to save me from what I'm about to do, I will find a slim envelope from Robyn in my department mailbox. Inside is a picture of a vest that she's clipped from a catalog. This vest is for fishing and it has many features, mesh panels and zippered pockets and an array of toggles. "Remember," she has written on it, "you are not invested."

The Vest falters, briefly losing momentum, and the only woman who has been at the university longer than I have begins to speak. She's trying to bring the meeting back around to business. Excuse me, The Vest says curtly, could you please let me finish? He continues, at length. I check my watch. I close my notebook. I cough. Nobody looks at me except The Vest. I mouth silently at him, "I want to kill you." I'm appalled at myself, but I use his confused pause as an opportunity to interrupt. I don't talk long because the meeting, he decides, is over.

BARTLEBY

Every year financial advisers come to campus to meet with faculty, but I haven't met with one until now. He's looking over the details of my retirement account with concern. Is there a reason, he asks me, why none of it has been invested in the stock market for the past decade?

"A Story of Wall-Street" is the subtitle to Melville's "Bartleby the Scrivener." Bartleby was a passive resister, a worker who refused to do certain work at first, then refused to work at all, and finally refused even to be fired, all by saying politely, "I would prefer not to." His resistance had no end, and he didn't seem to be trying to accomplish anything except resistance. I remind myself that Bartleby starved to death in prison, because somehow his story still reads to me as a triumph. Jane Desmarais writes, "Bartleby's freedoms are incompatible with life."

Like Bartleby, I would prefer not to. I would prefer not to be told what to do and I would prefer not to invest in the stock market. I would prefer not to put money into a system that extracts profit from other people's labor. That's one reason I chose the "no risk" option when I set up the account. But I don't tell the adviser this. I just say, I'm conservative. He looks skeptical. With money, I clarify.

Well, he says, moving some papers around, let's not talk about how much money you'd have now if you'd invested it. Let's just get the account in order. When do you want to retire? As soon as possible, I say. Most of the professors he advises plan to keep working well past the usual retirement age, he tells me. Yes, I know those professors. I work with them, or for them. I don't explain the difference between my job and theirs—the higher course load, the lower pay, the basement office, the glass ceiling. I just say, I'm not like them.

Then you're going to need to invest aggressively, he says. High risk, high return. He shows me a pie chart with stocks and bonds. He's talking about various kinds of investment now, index funds and hedge funds and options and futures. I ask, halfheartedly, what futures are. His explanation doesn't clarify much, but I didn't expect it to. I can tell that he doesn't entirely understand all the intricacies of this business himself. I wonder, silently, if I might actually be buying other people's futures.

This financial adviser works for the Teachers Insurance and Annuity Association, which I've only ever known as TIAA, the place where retirement money goes. It was established a hundred years ago by Andrew Carnegie, who sold his steel company to J. P. Morgan and became the richest man in America. TIAA is the largest agricultural investor in the world, the third largest commercial real estate manager in the world, and number 80 on the Fortune 500.

Now my money is out there, being aggressive. I keep thinking about it, wondering what it's doing. I consider calling the financial adviser to tell him that I would prefer not to be aggressive. I decide I will, and then I don't.

INVESTMENT

The bank regulator who lives across the street wants the house kitty-corner to mine "shut down." There was a shooting in the alley last week and two of the shooters, teenage boys, ran into that house. Nobody was hurt, but there was a scene with the police. When John and J came back from playing basketball in the park, our block was taped off and police officers holding guns were standing on our lawn talking to the boys in the house through megaphones.

I thought this neighborhood was safe, a mother at the playground complains to me. She and I both moved here from the same neighborhood in Chicago. That neighborhood wasn't considered safe and it's not far away. We don't get out of living with what everyone else lives with, I think, just because we own houses now. We can't buy our way out of shootings. I'm impatient with this conversation and with her illusion of safety. This wasn't the only shooting in our neighborhood this year, it was just the closest.

The bank regulator barely lives here. He works in two other cities and there's usually nobody in his big house on the double lot. He's the least likely person on this block, I say, to get hit by a stray bullet. He's not concerned about his safety, John says, he's concerned about his property. That house is an investment, and the value just went down $5,000 at least.

The bank regulator sends a text to the neighbors and organizes a meeting while I'm away for work. The chief of police comes to the meeting and says that it isn't legal to force an eviction. Everyone seems to agree, a neighbor tells me, that you can't just shut down a household. Even so, a month later I watch the people who live there carrying their things out to a U-Haul. I watch this the way I might watch bad weather—as if it has nothing to do with me.

Now I'm in my attic in the dark and I see the bank regulator's shadow projected by the security lights on his lawn into the mist of the night. His shadow is stretching through the trees, sending long fingers across the street. I've seen this scene before, in a black-and-white Dracula movie. I recall the workingwoman, the typist, who was Dracula's neighbor in London. He forced her to drink his blood, which gave her access to his mind. She was able to track his every move because she could see what he was seeing, as if she were looking through his eyes. And she knew she had to destroy him to save her own soul because she felt herself becoming a vampire.

WELCOME TO THE JUNGLE

I pass the Woman's Club, with its Grecian columns, every day on my way to work, but I've never been inside it until now. Sara thought that it might be fun, or funny, for us to attend the annual revue at the Woman's Club. We don't know what a revue is, but we know the club is raising funds to support book groups for pregnant teenagers in Chicago.

The revue, it turns out, involves the members of the Woman's Club dancing and singing onstage. One of the opening numbers features women dressed as slices of cake singing about resisting the temptation to eat, their thin thighs in black pantyhose extending from the cake around their torsos. All this is set, strangely, to the tune of Meghan Trainor's "No." And then there's "Landscape Disaster," a song that pretends to be about competing with the neighbors to have the trimmest hedge while its true subject is the proper grooming of pubic hair.

These women, John will remind me later, came of age in the sororities and clubs of elite colleges, where some really weird shit goes on. There were no sororities at my college and our only dance was a drag ball. What's weird to me is that this show seems to be a satire of the lives of wealthy women from another era, set to contemporary pop music. The past is dancing with the present and singing slightly out of tune. There's a song about belonging to a sewing circle. And a song about becoming bored in painting classes that were intended to stave off boredom. I feel dragged back into the age of corsets and suffrage and temperance.

Our local brewery is called Temperance, and the house of a temperance crusader, Frances Willard, is on the same block as the Woman's Club. I think of it as the Museum of Good Intentions. Willard fought for the eight-hour workday and the vote for women while also fighting for the prohibition of alcohol. "Do everything" was her slogan. Willard served as the first dean of women at the university where I teach. The president of the university then was a man to whom she had once been engaged but had not married. She remained unmarried and went on to become president of the Woman's Christian Temperance Union. Willard was an unconventional woman, "lesbian-like" in her attachments to other women. But she had a public feud with Ida B. Wells, who accused her of inciting lynching after she said that one of the dangers of alcohol was the rape of white women by black men. The popular belief that white mobs lynched black men in defense of women was an "old threadbare lie," Wells explained, a lie that obscured the true purpose of lynching—the violent control of black people.

Now the women are performing a song set to the tune of "You Don't Own Me." I think about how the original song lives on in the parody like a palimpsest, the trace of text remaining on a page that has been erased. Like the past living in the present, the blithe racism of wealthy women still not erased from the feminism of our time.

Sometimes the underwritten text is more legible than what's been written over it. "Welcome to the Jungle," a song from my adolescence, now has the chorus *Welcome to the gun show*. Women in leotards carrying cardboard barbells help me understand that this is not a song about the NRA. But it might be about aggression. Or maybe what I'm hearing in my mind, not quite erased, are Axl Rose's original lyrics: *Uh, I, I want to watch you bleed*. And, *You're gonna die.*

What's the jungle? I'm still wondering the day after the show. If there's a narrative in the lyrics of that song, it's the story of a woman being introduced through drug addiction to the violence of the street. The jungle is the street. The street that one can look down on, safely, from a treadmill in the health club.

I'm thinking about this in the locker room of the health club where I'm changing into my swimsuit when I hear some women on the other side of the lockers talking about how tired they are from performing in the fundraiser last night. These women and I belong, I realize, to the same club.

MAINTENANCE

I'm trimming the hedge in front of my house using hand shears. We sold the electric clippers that came with the house at a garage sale and I regret it now. When we sold the clippers we had just been to France, where I visited Notre-Dame and saw three men trimming the hedges. They were using hand shears and a wooden form that fit over the hedge as a guide. Their work was slow and silent and beautiful. I didn't go into Notre-Dame, I just stood outside watching the hedges be trimmed by hand.

Later, I went to see the catacombs but the line was too long, so I didn't go in. Instead, I stood outside the metro station and watched three men laying paving stones on the sidewalk. One of them brushed sand between the stones, and one poured water over the sand, and one tamped it down with an iron rod. That morning, I began my day sitting at a sidewalk café eating a croissant while I watched a woman reaching out her arm from a dark interior to clean all the windows on the third floor of the building across the street.

When Mierle Laderman Ukeles scrubbed the front steps of the Wadsworth Atheneum Museum of Art on her hands and knees, what she was doing was not work but art. Or it was both, and that was the point. She wanted to close the distance between work and art. "This is early feminism, very rigid," she said later, "I literally was divided in two. Half of my week I was the mother, and the other half the artist. But, I thought to myself, 'this is ridiculous, I am the one.'"

My working will be the work, she proposed in her "Manifesto for Maintenance Art 1969!" She wrote: *Clean your desk, wash the dishes, clean the floor, wash your clothes, wash your toes, change the baby's diaper, finish the report, correct the typos, mend the fence . . . go to work, this art is dusty, clear the table, call him again, flush the toilet, stay young.*

Middle age is really all about maintenance, my mother once said. I was a teenager when she said this and I was helping her scrape the peeling paint off her house, which would later burn down. You spend your life accumulating things, she said, and then you have to maintain them. Your house, your car, your body. You have to maintain your children, too, and your parents.

This seemed sadder to me then than it does now. I don't like trimming the hedges, but I feel anchored by the chore. Maintenance is the tax I pay on this life, I think. And that is why I want to do it by hand, with heavy shears.

Maintenance is a drag; it takes all the fucking time, Ukeles wrote in her manifesto. And then she dedicated her career to it. Maintenance, she wrote, was the work of protecting progress, sustaining change, preserving the new, and keeping the dust off invention. Then, as now, the work of invention, of making something new, and of generating change was more highly valued than the work of maintenance. And more highly paid. Art, in that moment, was in the process of reinventing itself. Art was new, work unlike any other work.

In a work called *Touch Sanitation Performance*, Ukeles spent eleven months tracking down every one of New York's 8,500 sanitation workers, shaking their hands, and telling each one of them: "Thank you for keeping New York City alive!" During her eight-hour and sixteen-hour shifts, or "sweeps," she shadowed sanitation workers, interviewed them, and listened to their complaints. In Staten Island, they said: "Do you know why everybody hates us? They think we're their mother. They think we're their maid."

In another work, her subject was the three hundred maintenance workers in the building where her artwork was to be shown. She spent five weeks approaching workers, taking Polaroid photos of them, and asking them if they would call what they were doing work or art. She was underscoring the

fact that some people get to call their work art and others
have to just do their work. She put their photos and their
answers on exhibit, and when the workers came to see the
exhibit, it was the first time they had visited the museum in
the building they maintained. But her work didn't close the
distance between her art and their work. Just as my work
doesn't close the distance between me and my neighbors.

As I back up to see the shape of the hedge, I'm aware of a
woman standing next to a suitcase on the front lawn of the
house kitty-corner to mine. She's shouting at a man in a car
that's idling at the curb. Something like this happens fairly
often over there. They have an overgrown hedge, and no tools
or time to trim it. When the people who rent that house are
outside, I feel embarrassed to be trimming my hedge. Don't
mind me, I think, I'm just tending my assets.

SIN STOCKS

I'm meeting with a financial adviser again, a different one this time. He's talking about diversification, describing how broadly he will invest my retirement money, not just in large corporations like Amazon, but in midsize and small corporations, and not just in the United States, but in Russia and China. It will be in a wide range of industries, too, not just manufacturing, but emerging technologies and real estate and other things.

I ask him if there's any way to know exactly what I own. He doesn't buy individual stocks for me, he explains, he selects mutual funds, which are hundreds of stocks bundled together by professional money managers in New York, who are themselves choosing from stocks that have been curated by other money people who monitor the performance of stocks flagged by other money people. I'm far removed from anyone who knows anything about the companies I've bought into.

If I want, the adviser says, I can avoid certain "sin stocks." Some mutual funds are designed to exclude companies that make their profits on alcohol, tobacco, gambling, or weapons. Maybe, he suggests, gambling doesn't bother me, but I'd like to avoid directly investing in fossil fuels. That's possible, to some extent. Or maybe I want to invest in companies that treat their workers well. I'll have to choose a priority, he says, because the same company that offers a generous maternity leave might do something destructive to the environment. This is the moral hazard of diversification.

Investment isn't any more of a sin, I think, than gambling. But when shareholders profit at the expense of the workers who produce those profits, it's a means of extraction. An economy of extraction is what we're retiring on, those of us who get to retire. Amazon has stopped giving stock to hundreds of thousands of employees, while Jeff Bezos owns 16 percent of the company, making him the richest man in the world. His workers, who are tracked electronically to increase their efficiency in hot warehouses, have an injury rate higher than loggers. And the terms of their employment are worse than they would have been fifty years ago. "If Amazon's 575,000 total employees owned the same proportion of their employer's stock as the Sears workers did in the 1950s, they would each own shares worth $381,000," write Nelson Schwartz and Michael Corkery. "This shift is broader than a single company's culture. . . . In many cases publicly traded companies are concentrating wealth, not spreading it." I want nothing to do with this, I think. But I want to retire.

The adviser is assuring me now that even if the market dips, even if it crashes, it will come back up again. Given time, he says, it always comes back. I ask him if he can imagine this system of investment coming to an end. No, he says, your money is safe. But that's not what I'm asking. I'm asking if there's any way out of this.

INTEGRITY

There's a statue of a woman with her arms outstretched on the front of the New York Stock Exchange, Eric tells me. The title of this statue is *Integrity Protecting the Works of Man*.

Eric was my student, many years ago, and now he's writing a book about air-conditioning, which is really a book about how our comfort is destroying our world. The more comfortable we are, research suggests, the more destruction we are likely to be causing. No matter how much you care about the world, no matter how conscious you are, the best predictor of your impact on the environment is your income.

The first complete, working air-conditioning system was installed in the New York Stock Exchange, which is what gave Eric an excuse to ask for a tour of the trading floor. At first, his request was denied—too much of a security risk—but he tried again. Granted access and cleared by security, he was met by a historian who guided him down a series of corridors and stairs to the main trading floor. They talked about air-conditioning, so it was hard to avoid talking about politics. Air-conditioning, Eric tells me, is always political.

Air-conditioning is where the economist Mariana Mazzucato turned her attention when she was among a group of experts advising the United Nations on sustainability. They were meeting in an overcooled room, so she asked for the air-conditioning to be turned off. How can we hope to change anything, she asked, "if we don't rebel in the everyday?"

The way we think about value is one of the things Mazzucato would like to change. Our understanding of value, she observes, is circular. "Incomes are justified by the production of something that is of value. But how do we measure value? By whether it earns income." And so, "the concept of *unearned income* vanishes." If we could think about value differently, we could modify our economic system so that something of value to our entire society, like the well-being of our children or the preservation of our environment, would also have economic value. Investment is essential, she argues. But we need to ask, "What are we investing *in*?"

The historian led Eric to a roped-off area and told him to stay within it. The trading floor was filled with men. The countdown to the bell began. It was a round, flat bell, like the fire alarm bells in public schools, but it was gold. Eric's view was blocked, so he could see only the bell, not the hand that rang it. It was, he tells me, the invisible hand of capitalism.

The bell rang, and it kept ringing. The only thing like it that he had ever experienced was the solar eclipse. The world went dark, crickets chirped, birds panicked. People around him were clapping and laughing. Tears came to his eyes, which embarrassed him, but nobody noticed. They were all looking at their phones. And this is how he got out of the stock exchange without being discovered as a spy.

SPY VS. SPY

I'm lost in Chicago. I was on my way to pick up David but I was listening to a radio program about Navajo code talkers and I got distracted thinking about what it might have felt like to use your native language to help defend the country that had confined that language to a reservation.

J is reading *Spy vs. Spy* comics and crying when we get back to the house. I ask him why he's crying and he says, Because the song is so sad. He shows me a panel of the comic where the white spy is whistling a few musical notes and the black spy is crying. There is no sad song, there is just the idea of a sad song. J's tears don't make sense to me, but I don't think the Cold War politics of *Spy vs. Spy* make sense to him. He must be reading his own story into the submarine in the bathtub and the bomb under the bed. It's a violent comic, but what I like about it is that nobody ever wins.

David tells us that he's been watching a TV show called *The Americans*, about two Russian spies who pose as an American family in the suburbs during the Cold War. They have real children who are not spies, just children, and they live in a real house, but they work fake jobs and report back to the KGB.

That's how I feel, I tell David, I feel like a spy faking this life. Me too, John says. But why, I wonder? And who do we think we're spying on—we're just like everyone else who lives around here. No, John says, we're nothing like them, I'm nothing like them.

APOCALYPSE NOW

It's the Fourth of July in our backyard and John drove all the
way down to Indiana for fireworks. I watch him position an
alarmingly large rocket in a bucket full of rock salt. The rocket seems to be aimed at our house. At work the other day,
one of our colleagues told me that he'd seen John riding his
bike without a helmet. Yes, I told him, John doesn't always
wear a helmet. He doesn't wear sunscreen either, and sometimes he doesn't wear his seat belt. It's an aesthetic, I explained.

I could also have said that it's a critique, an embodied critique
of the middle-class cult of personal safety. It's a rejection of
the belief that every vulnerability should be protected, and
that the central project of our lives is to undo our own precarity. It's a refusal of a way of life devoted to insurance.

I won't buy our son out of an uncertain future, John says when
we discuss life insurance. That's what life is, he says. I don't
want to argue with that. Instead, I quietly submit a blood

sample and sign the paperwork that will insure my life for $250,000.

There were fireworks at my cousin's wedding, an amateur show like this one. She'd brewed her own hard cider and raised her own pig to roast. A few months later her husband was dead, killed by a falling tree. He was a logger and the tree that killed him was called a widow-maker because he wasn't the first young man to die that way. He had no insurance, as insurance wouldn't cover work that dangerous.

Maybe what we're celebrating is not independence, but precarity. The closeness of the match to the explosive. I watch my son light the fuse on a smoke bomb and huge yellow plumes waft across the lawn in front of the garage. The smoke hangs in the humid air, thick and acrid. Our backyard looks like the set for *Apocalypse Now*. Saigon, John says, shit.

GREAT AMERICA

Ray took his children to an amusement park, John tells me, where tickets cost $75 for adults and $55 for children. For an extra $100 per person, he could buy tickets that would allow him to cut in line. He could walk past other families, all of whom had also bought tickets, and go right to the front of the line and get on a ride. If he liked that ride, he could stay on and ride again while those other families continued to wait in the heat with their children watching him take another ride. This felt wrong, Ray said, but it was worth it. His only other choice was to watch other people cut in line.

Do you know what this place is called, John asks, where a person can buy a ticket like this? Great America. The technology that makes line cutting possible at Great America was invented by an Englishman, and it is contracted out to American amusement parks by a British company. John learned this from an essay by Tom Junod. The British import of line cutting, Junod notes, is "perfectly in keeping with the two-tiering of America."

Junod takes his daughter to a waterpark every year for the lines. There, people wait wet and undressed, in camaraderie, with their scars and their tattoos exposed. "They're a vision not just of democracy in action but democracy unveiled," Junod writes of the lines, "a glimpse of what the last line is going to look like, when all is revealed, and we're waiting for our interview with Saint Peter." Buying a ticket that allows cutting, he observes, amounts to paying to degrade other people's experience. If some people don't stand in line at all, then other people have to stand in line longer. Which, as any child can see, is unfair.

I've just read that the five wealthiest people in this country have more money than the bottom 50 percent combined, I tell John. This, he says, is not a democracy.

Now we're watching *The Americans* and they're arguing about defecting. The husband suggests that if they sold out to the FBI, they could get enough money to live a comfortable life in the US. They could have reliable electricity and plenty of closet space. The good life, he says. But the wife doesn't want this life.

He knows that it kills her, the husband says, to see their children becoming American. She's not done with them, she says, they're going to be different. Not communists, maybe, but socialists.

This country, the husband says, doesn't turn out socialists.

CAPITALISM

The only TV show J ever watches is *Scooby-Doo*. Other TV shows scare him. *Scooby-Doo* features ghosts and mummies and vampires, but it's a comedy about fear. Scooby and Shaggy quake to a laugh track.

There were only two seasons and twenty-five episodes of the original *Scooby-Doo, Where Are You!* series, and J has watched all of them several times before I learn that this series was conceived in response to parents who protested violent cartoons in the 1960s. It was originally titled *Who's S-S-Scared?*, a question that may have been aimed at those pacifist parents. Watching it now, I realize with surprise that *Scooby-Doo* is all about capitalism. Every ghost, every mummy, every vampire turns out, in the end, to be someone trying to get rich.

In one episode, the gang are on vacation in Hawaii, where they learn from the owner of a newspaper that a nearby village is haunted. After being chased by a witch doctor and passing through a series of trapdoors, trick walls, and secret entrances, they discover that the witch doctor is the newspaperman, who has been trying to scare the villagers away so that he can poach their pearl beds.

Another episode features the ghost of a miner who can't rest until he finds the last vein of gold in an abandoned mine. There are trip lines in this episode, too, and trapdoors, and Scooby and Shaggy are frightened by a player piano, until Velma explains that "it's not haunted, it's automatic." The ghost of the miner turns out to be a man who has discovered oil in the gold mine. "Not gold," Velma clarifies, "black gold." He is trying to scare all the guests away from the local hotel so that he can buy the hotel and the mine.

I tell all this to the father standing next to me on the playground, who says, Well, it's about dysfunctional capitalism, right? Capitalism gone wrong. People who are trying to game the system. He's a lawyer. Yes, I say, but isn't that how capitalism works? There's always got to be a trapdoor that allows the capitalist to access a profit greater than the original investment. As I say this, I wonder if I'm describing capitalism or the paranoia that life within capitalism produces.

TITANIC

Robyn gives me a cup of tea in which the *Titanic* is sinking. This tiny *Titanic* holds loose tea, but when I look at it, canted dangerously with just a bit of hull still above water, it seems to be filled not with tea, but with tiny oak furniture sliding across tiny ballroom floors, and tiny china breaking against tiny grand pianos.

I once met a woman, an heiress to a cemetery fortune, who kept a piece of china from the *Titanic* in a glass cabinet. It seemed like a strange artifact to display. That woman was a flutist who performed all over the world, her music financed by real estate for the dead.

The *Titanic* was the product of competition between three luxury lines, first to build the fastest ship and then to build the biggest ship. There were not enough lifeboats on the *Titanic* for all the passengers, but there were more than required by the regulations of the time, which seems like a familiar story. "If I had had a brimful glass of water in my hand not a drop would have been spilled," one survivor recalled of the moment the ship hit the iceberg. Perhaps we should all keep a memento of the *Titanic*, just to remind ourselves of how safe disaster feels.

The owner of Macy's was on the *Titanic*, and so was Benjamin Guggenheim, who famously dressed for his death. The rose in his buttonhole is less remarkable to me than the fact that he stayed with his valet, who was dark-skinned. They went down sitting on deck chairs together, sipping brandy and smoking cigars. A hundred years later, his family gave me $45,000 to write a book.

I sip my tea, imagining rich people drowning in the very water I'm drinking, though most of the dead, I know, were third class. I think of the odd pleasure I took in that scene in the movie where water floods the ballroom and roils up the grand staircase. It was the pleasure of seeing wealth come to ruin. A pleasure that lives, strangely, right next to the pleasures of wealth.

REPEAT

John and I are standing on a sidewalk in Chicago, examining a menu that lists one hundred varieties of whiskey. The problem of having too much to drink is, for me, a new problem. I recall with some nostalgia the years when I had only one beer a week, at most. And tell me, John says, were you happy then?

Shortly after I moved to New York I discovered the repeat function on my roommate's stereo and played "The Thrill Is Gone" over and over until she made me stop. I was feeling blue and that was the only blues in our collection. When she wasn't around I played Brian Eno and cried. *I'll find a place somewhere in the corner / I'm gonna waste the rest of my days.* Only someone who is going through something, my cousin observed, plays songs on repeat. I was twenty-two and the thrill was gone—I was going to waste the rest of my days. I know now that this is funny, but I had no sense of humor then. I sat by my window, looking out over bricks and concrete while the lyrics turned hopefully toward the garden gate. I didn't

have a garden or a garden gate, I had a wall marked by my bicycle tire. I was living off $10,000 a year and I didn't qualify
for Medicaid. When I wasn't nursing heartbreak to the tune
of Brian Eno, I was preoccupied with what I was going to do
for work. I was going through something, yes. And now I'm
through it, I think, and going through something else.

ART

David comes over, bringing a painting for us from his office wall. The painting is based on one of his poems, which was based on a movie. Last year John made a video based on David's latest book, which was based on a television series, which was based on a novel. This is how art eats, I think—it feeds itself with art.

We're paging through a book of photographs that John brought home from the library. John and I knew the woman who took these photographs, but this is the first time we've ever seen her work. She lived out her last days on a bench in the park across from our apartment, looking at the lake. We thought she was homeless but she wasn't. John spoke French with her and they talked about the poems John had memorized when he worked as a nanny in France. I didn't talk to her, as she only ever yelled at me. Get a hat, she would yell when she saw me in the park bareheaded. Get a bell, she would yell when she saw me with my bike. When an ambulance took her away from the bench in the park I still didn't know her name.

I'm trying to explain to David why I haven't seen either of the movies about her and why I haven't read any of the books. It felt wrong—her resurrection as a mythic artist so soon after she'd been sitting on a bench eating from a can. Her photographs were acquired by a real estate agent while she was still alive, when she could no longer make payments on her storage locker and its contents were auctioned off. Her death two years later was convenient for the real estate agent, in that it allowed her work to become a product unfettered by the troublesome person who made it.

Like Darger, David says, and maybe also Dickinson.

I tell him about the "Narrative of Her Captivity," the title I've given in my mind to a twenty-page account written by a neighbor of mine who once employed this photographer as a nanny. I've titled it after Mary Rowlandson's account of her time held captive by Native Americans, as my neighbor seems to have felt captive, in a way, to the photographer, whom she considered strange and somewhat savage. For three years in the 1980s the photographer lived in the attic of my neighbor's house and cared for her three children. She was in her late fifties then and had already taken many hundreds of photographs.

When she negotiated her salary, which was $175 a week, the photographer mentioned that she had to live. My neighbor, her employer, wondered what she meant by that—what more could she need beyond room and board? The photographer also wanted a lock on her door. Her employer wondered why a door wasn't enough. "A room," Virginia Woolf had taken care to specify, "with a lock on the door."

The photographer's first job had been in a sweatshop in Manhattan. She sewed well and she liked nice fabrics. She bought her skirts and jackets at thrift stores, but then she had them altered and dry-cleaned, which was expensive. Maybe this, her employer speculated, was what she meant when she said she had to live. She kept twelve broken Leica cameras in storage.

She asked if she could take the *New York Times* upstairs to her room. That wasn't all she asked. She asked for more pay in exchange for more housework, but her employer refused. Then her employer unlocked the door to her room and discovered that the photographer had piled up years of newspapers in there—her room was full of them. Before she was fired, they had an argument in which the photographer said they were her newspapers and her employer reminded her that, no, they weren't.

What made her famous, after her death, is that she had saved, in addition to newspapers, all her rolls of undeveloped film and all the negatives of all her photographs. But in the end those weren't hers either.

ONE'S OWN

"Women have always been poor," Virginia Woolf wrote in *A Room of One's Own*. Denied education, excluded from professions, and unable to own property, even rich women were poor, in a way. British women had just been given the vote in 1929, while the fictional narrator of *A Room of One's Own* had just inherited some money. The money, she insisted, was more important than the vote. When she wrote this, Woolf was enjoying her first commercial success as a writer and earning a substantial income for the first time—"This last half year I made over £1800," she noted in her diary, "almost at the rate of £4000 a year, the salary almost of a Cabinet minister." She was using that money, the proceeds from her most recent book, to build an addition on her house, a room for writing.

That was at her country house, not her house in London. She didn't really want for rooms. But in London she wrote in a basement storage room surrounded by stacks of books from the press she ran with Leonard. In the 1920s, their combined annual income of £1,100 was modest compared to, say, a law-yer's income, but they were still comfortably middle class. They paid their live-in cook, Nellie Boxall, £50 per year, less than the average rate for a cook, and Nellie argued that she ought to be paid more. In addition to preparing all their meals, Nellie cleaned and dusted, washed dishes, did some laundry, hauled coal, and polished boots. She worked for Virginia for eighteen years and was her only servant for ten of those years. Through it all they argued.

They argued about Nellie's refusal to make marmalade and they argued about Virginia's refusal to raise Nellie's pay. They argued over the unexpected guests who dropped by for im-promptu dinner parties, which added shopping and baking to Nellie's work. If Nellie had her friends then she should have hers, Virginia reasoned, blind to the difference, which was that she didn't cook for Nellie's friends or wash their dishes. From time to time, Nellie would quit in protest, but then she would revoke her notice as soon as Virginia began to look for her replacement.

The argument that ended it all was an argument that took place in Nellie's room just after Virginia published *A Room of One's Own*. In anger, Nellie told Virginia to get out of her room. It was as if she had slapped her. Virginia had been given an order by her own servant. And Nellie had called the room where she slept "my room." It was Virginia's room—she owned it.

"Intellectual freedom depends upon material things," she wrote in *A Room of One's Own*. Things like housing and food. Yes, the room was symbolic, she allowed, and the lock on the door was the power to think for oneself. But she meant it literally, too. In order to write, a woman needed the space and time to do her work, and she needed money. She needed £500 per year, to be precise, the equivalent of £75,000 today. Alison Light writes, "Very few women could expect that level of income in 1929, unless, like Virginia, from invested capital, and a full-time job at this salary would hardly provide the freedom to write."

Virginia fired Nellie after the argument in Nellie's room, but then she lost her resolve and took her back, though she didn't forget "the famous scene." She wrote, "I am always seeing myself told to 'leave my room.'" Nellie fell seriously ill and spent some months in the hospital before she was fired for good. "After eighteen years I at last got rid of an affectionate domestic tyrant," Virginia wrote. She felt freed, as if it were she, Virginia, who had been in service to Nellie. She had always disliked her dependence on Nellie, and Nellie's dependence on her. Their mutual bondage. When she fired her, she felt "executioner & the executed in one." She could confuse herself with Nellie in her mind, but she could not allow Nellie a room of her own.

GUGGENHEIM

I have my own office now, after ten years at the university. It is brand-new and freshly painted. A man with an electric screwdriver stops by to hang a coat hook behind the door. I mention the gift a donor has just given the university and he knows the fundraising target, $3.75 billion, and the amount of the gift, $100 million. Where did that money come from? he wonders. Nowhere good, I say, though it's obvious I know less about this than he does. He's quiet for a moment while he backs up to inspect his work. Then he says, No, I can't think of any way that kind of money could come from something good.

I wondered, when I got a grant from the Guggenheim Foundation, where the money came from. But I avoided finding out until after I had spent it. I bought a new bicycle and I paid the university for each course I didn't teach while I was writing. "Buying out" is the term for this, the opportunity to buy back my own time—a luxury most jobs don't afford. The time

I spent writing cost me $22,000 one year and $22,000 again the next year.

It was mining money—silver in Colorado, gold in the Yukon, diamonds in the Belgian Congo, and diamonds in Angola. It took two generations to amass this fortune, one of the biggest in the world, extracted from the earth and smelted out of human labor. In 1925, a fraction of that fortune was set aside so that artists and scholars could apply, each year, for an allotment.

John Simon Guggenheim, who established the grants, was the chief ore buyer for his father's company. His brother Solomon collected art and funded the museum in New York. And his brother Benjamin died on the *Titanic*. Benjamin's daughter Peggy inherited $450,000, which was a small inheritance for a Guggenheim. She took a job as an unpaid clerk for an avant-garde bookstore in New York before she went to Paris, where she met the avant-garde. She opened a gallery in London that lost money. And then she decided to build a collection. "I put myself on a regime to buy one picture a day," she wrote. It was work, her collecting.

She bought ten Picassos, forty Ernsts, eight Mirós, four Magrittes, three Man Rays, three Dalís, one Klee, and one Chagall. As the Germans advanced on Paris she was buying paintings from artists desperate to leave the country. During the occupation, she hid her collection in a barn because the Louvre didn't think it was worth saving. The art she collected didn't matter yet, which is what made it an affordable investment.

I keep returning to a photograph of her in a dress that seems to be made of cellophane. She's in Paris, with Notre-Dame outside the window behind her and a painting by Miró on the wall. It's around 1930, so she has already met Marcel Duchamp and Scott Fitzgerald and Alfred Stieglitz and seen the work of Cézanne and Picasso and Matisse. She's met Djuna Barnes and given her money. But she hasn't yet met Beckett at a party thrown by Joyce and spent the night in bed with him. She hasn't slept with all the artists she will sleep with. And she hasn't yet begun sending monthly checks for $150 to Jackson Pollock, which will allow him to quit his job as a janitor at her uncle's museum. Her first great accomplishment, she will later say, was Pollock, and her second was her collection.

I stare at her, wondering about accomplishment, hers and mine, and how much it has to do with money. I would not have a house if not for the Guggenheim, I know that much. My down payment would have been spent on time to write. It wasn't a gift, John says. I thought of it, when it came, as payment for my work. But it wasn't that either. It was an investment.

CAPITALISM

Using money to get more money, I tell my father, is David Graeber's definition of capitalism. I'm a bad capitalist, my father says. I am too, though I seem to be getting better. It's the way we were raised, my father suggests. He was raised Catholic, but I was not.

Historically, the Catholic Church didn't approve of the "breeding" of money, the making of money from money. Neither did Aristotle, Islam, or the Quakers. Aristotle's complaint was that money made from money was unproductive, in that nothing was produced except more money. But Aristotle didn't consider productive work a moral duty the way the Church would later. Time spent working, he argued, is time not spent on things that improve a person, like the pursuit of truth through study.

The Old Testament forbade lending money for interest unless the loan was made to a stranger: "Thou shalt not lend upon usury to thy brother" but "unto a stranger thou mayest lend upon usury." Jews could not charge interest from other Jews, but they could from Christians, who qualified as strangers. Early Judaism was unique, Maristella Botticini and Zvi Eckstein argue, in that it required Jewish men to read, to study the Torah, and to send their sons to school. Literacy was rare back then, in part because it was not particularly useful for farming, but it equipped Jews to write contracts and keep accounts. Literate Jews left agriculture, over the course of centuries, and established themselves as moneylenders in Europe long before they were excluded from other professions. The unproductive work of moneylending allowed for a life devoted to study.

The New Testament implored Christians to give their money away. As Luke put it, "Lend, hoping for nothing again." A gift, an act of charity, was morally superior to a loan. But usury, officially forbidden by the medieval Church, was still practiced, particularly by monks. In the twelfth century, Christians began to replace Jews as lenders to kings and popes and wealthy clergy, while Jews were confined to lending on the village level, where they drew the resentment of the indebted poor. And so, Benjamin Nelson writes, two types of moneylenders emerged, one reviled and one admired: "the degraded manifest usurer-pawnbroker, as often as not a Jew; and the city father, arbiter of elegance, patron of the arts, devout philanthropist, the merchant prince."

I'm doubly entangled in moneylending, as I have both a mortgage and a retirement account. I pay interest on a loan that allows me to live in a house, itself an investment, while I invest my excess income in the stock market, breeding money for future use. Capitalism, Lewis Hyde writes, is "the ideology that asks that we remove surplus wealth from circulation and lay it aside to produce more wealth." The defining feature of capitalism, he suggests, is not the breeding of money, but the hoarding of money for that purpose.

Hoarding money is not generally considered miserly these days so much as it is considered necessary. Hoarding, in the form of savings and investments, is regarded as sound economic practice, smart, and morally upright. Private investment provides security for the privileged class—covering the expenses of education and illness and old age—in a country that lacks public investment in security. But our political structure is not the only one given to hoarding.

"It is quite possible," Hyde notes, "to have the state own everything and still convert all gifts to capital, as Stalin demonstrated." Stalin funded his five-year plan by exporting grain from collective farms while the farmers who produced those profits starved. And so, "to move away from capitalism is not to change the form of ownership from the few to the many, but to cease turning so much surplus into capital, that is, to treat most increase as a gift."

I wonder what this really means, in a lived life—to treat most increase as a gift. I think of Toni Morrison and the women she lived among in Queens in the seventies. She was a single mother supporting two young children, but she'd send a check, a "grant," to another woman writer, say Toni Cade Bambara, whenever she made some extra money freelancing. And Toni Cade Bambara, or someone else, might show up at her house with groceries, unasked, and cook dinner.

A gift, Hyde writes, must keep moving. A gift must always be given away again, or something else must be given away in its place. There are tribal people, he writes, who have sayings like "One man's gift must not be another man's capital." Among the Uduk in northeast Africa, if a pair of goats is given as a gift, those goats must be eaten, not bred. If they are bred to make more goats, and thus transformed into capital, the person who has bred them will be expected to suffer some misfortune.

"In folk tales," Hyde observes, "the person who tries to hold on to a gift usually dies."

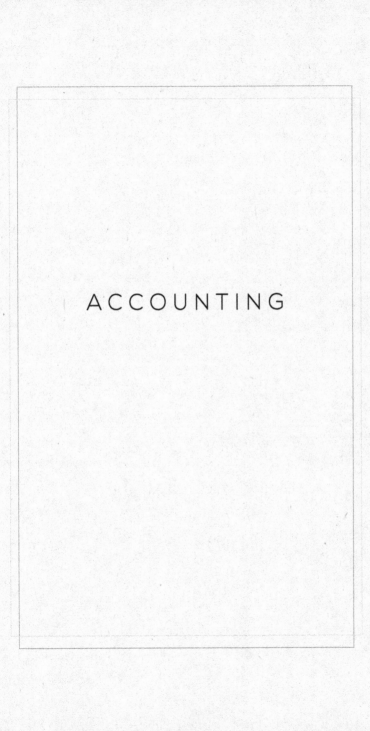

ACCOUNTING

ART

I've been waiting all this time on the wrong platform and the train just sped by in the wrong direction. The first drops of rain are falling now and I see a taxi idling under the tracks. The driver is an older man in a baby-blue suit and he wants to talk.

What do you think, he asks me, of art painted by elephants? If you're asking if I think it could be beautiful, I tell him, then I think it could, even if the elephant had no intention of making something beautiful. But if you're asking if abstract art isn't really art because it could be made by animals or children, then that's another question. What did you study in college? he asks. He studied architecture, but there wasn't any work for him when he graduated, with debt. And that's how he became a taxi driver. It's good work, he tells me, in that it pays the bills.

Do you think it's wrong, he asks, to make your living teaching something that won't earn your students a living? No, I say.

And then I pause over why. The service I'm doing for my students, I tell him, is teaching them how to find value in something that isn't widely valued. And I think it's a gift to give another person permission to do something worthless.

But I'm aware that what makes my job a "good" job is that I work at an elite university, where my pay is relatively high and my teaching load is relatively low and my students are already well educated. Many of them are also already rich. And if they aren't rich, they're likely to leave with debt. Debt that, yes, can't be paid off with anything I teach.

I've just been to a talk by the author of *Debt to Society: Accounting for Life under Capitalism*. After the talk, a woman in the audience said that it wasn't clear to her how her value to the university was determined—was it in the number of students she taught, or how much they learned, or what kind of work she prepared them to do? None of the above, I thought. Our value as teachers is determined the same way the value of any commodity is determined, by the market. The surest way to get a raise is not to work harder or teach more students, but to be offered a better job at another university. This is how I came to make $20,000 more than John, working the same hours in the same position, teaching the same subject. I don't believe my work to be worth more than his, nor do I believe it to be worth less than the work of the professors who make over twice what I make. There is no system of accounting here that I want to internalize. In the final tabulation, what I value—the practice of art, the cultivation of care—doesn't even appear on the ledger, inside or outside the university. Art is freeing in this sense, in that it's unaccountable.

There's a poem by June Jordan, "Free Flight," where she writes about finding herself awake at night, hungry for something she doesn't have, making a list of things to do that starts with toilet paper. Then she asks, *is this poem on my list?* Followed by, *light bulbs lemons envelopes ballpoint refill / post office and zucchini / oranges no / it's not.*

Every year, I'm required to fill out a form for the university that lists my contributions and accomplishments. *polish shoes file nails coordinate tops and bottoms / lipstick control no / screaming I'm bored because / this is whoring away the hours of god's creation.* I list the classes I've taught, the theses I've mentored, the committees I've served on, the essays I've published, the talks and lectures I've delivered. But is this poem on my list? What I want to report is that I've done absolutely nothing of value and that is my accomplishment.

Finally, I ask the driver what he thinks. He says, I think it's wrong.

EAT A PEACH

I don't believe that you think what you do is worthless, my sister says. I don't. I just mean financially worthless. Writing poetry doesn't usually produce money, for most people. Free verse is doubly free, in that it is unfettered by meter and it has no market value. I can pass as a writer who is not a poet, and my writing sometimes has market value, but it has never paid the rent. The money I earn from writing is unpredictable, more like an occasional windfall than a salary. But I don't measure the worth of my work in dollars. You should clarify that, my sister says. Is it too scary? she asks. She's not talking to me, she's talking to her son, who is watching *James and the Giant Peach*.

"Eat a Peach" was the slogan John wrote for a banner that hung above a table of peaches in the local food co-op of the town where we met. He did marketing for the co-op until he quit to work on his writing. It's an Allman Brothers album, John explained when I laughed. I still think it's funny. Not just the slogan, hanging above a pile of ripe peaches, but the very idea of marketing peaches, which the slogan seemed to mock. Aren't peaches their own advertisement?

"The reward of art is not fame or success but intoxication," Cyril Connolly writes. "And that is why so many bad artists are unable to live without it." The value of what I do is that it makes me feel alive, I tell my sister. Even more than alive. She isn't satisfied with this. Art has value for people who aren't artists, she insists, you should explain that value. Is it too scary? she asks again.

I think it's inherently scary, I say, being inside the pit of a peach, rolling along, not knowing where you're going, getting carried across the ocean by birds. It's a life marked by uncertainty and absurdity, the life of an artist. Maybe the value of art, to artists and everyone else, is that it upends other value systems. Art unmakes the world made by work.

Do I dare to eat a peach? asks J. Alfred Prufrock in his love song. Do I dare to eat a peach, he asks, after indecisions and revisions, after toast and tea, after a life measured out in coffee spoons, and after having already asked, *Do I dare / Disturb the universe?*

Women shouldn't have to work for nothing, I tell my sister, and neither should artists, but I feel the way some women once felt about the Wages for Housework movement—if I were paid wages for the work of making art, then everything

I do would be monetized, everything I do would be subject
to the logic of this economy. And if art became my job, I'm
afraid that would disturb my universe. I would have nothing
unaccountable left in my life, nothing worthless, except for
my child.

My sister's son is shrieking now. She says, It's too scary!

ACCOUNTING

I'm considering adding up everything I've ever been paid for writing, starting with $35 for a poem published twenty years ago. After some hours spent sifting through all my check stubs and tax returns and royalty statements, I could know for sure if the amount I've just been offered for one book is, as I suspect, more than the total of what I've earned for all my writing over the past twenty years. But then, if I added it all up, I'd have to wonder what I did with that money.

Marx was once promised 3,000 francs for a book. That was more than twice the annual salary of an average worker at the time. He asked to be paid 1,500 francs up front, but then he didn't finish the book and couldn't return the money, which he had already spent. Marx made some calculations by hand on the back of that book contract, calculations that are reproduced on a postcard Mara sent to me. She signed only "M," and I momentarily wondered if the postcard was from Marx, sent from his grave. His math was messy, and the caption noted that "history's greatest economic theorist appears to have turned to schoolboy division and addition in order to understand the finances of the agreement. Perhaps in frustration, he seems to have finally resorted to tally marks when his other calculations went awry."

Income's Outcome is a project that began when the artist Danica Phelps made drawings of everything she did with the money in her bank account until that balance was spent down to zero. She drew her son putting a coin into a parking meter, her hands opening bills, boots on her feet, a scooter, her son pushing a grocery cart. When she sold each one of those drawings, she recorded the income and drew everything she did with that money. The drawings are full of bodies, rendered in long liquid lines, overlapping in embrace, and hands holding things, cookies and eggs and apples. "Each time a batch of drawings is sold," she says of the project, "it creates a window into my life where I draw what I spend money on until that money is gone and then the window closes."

Her art is an accounting. When a drawing sells, she records the income by painting a green stripe, a tally mark, for every dollar. Money spent is painted in red stripes. Credit is gray, as it occupies the gray area between earnings and expenses.

In 2012, she exhibited a series of twenty-five plywood panels covered in 350,000 red gouache stripes for the $350,000 she lost in the foreclosure of the home she had shared with another woman, her former lover. *The Cost of Love* was the title of this work, which included words drawn from a housing court ruling: "animosity," "eviction," "mortgage." When she bought the home, she hired assistants to help her paint the 627,000 gray stripes that represented the loan of $627,000. But when it foreclosed, she painted every red stripe herself, which took five months. "It's like letting go of the house, every single penny of it," she told a reporter. "And once I've painted it, it's gone."

Not all the drawings she made for *Income's Outcome* were good, in her opinion, but she had to keep them all because they were part of the financial record, which was also the body of work. And so she priced them according to how much she valued them as works of art. "When I started showing my work, I put the price right on the drawing," she said. "In my first exhibition, there were pieces ranging from $7 to $1,600, based on how much I liked the drawing." The determination of the price, as one gallery noted, was her "final aesthetic decision."

How much a work of art is worth is usually determined by the market, not the artist. As Barbara Bourland explains, "Market prices can be set with no money exchanged and no tax obligation: one dealer has a Warhol for sale, previous sale at, let's say, $1 million. He sets the auction minimum at $10 million; dealer two buys it for $10 million. The record of value is set. At the same time, dealer two sells a similar work, from the same period, in a private sale to dealer number one, for the record-set price of $10 million. The net change is $0, but they have created, for the public record, a $10 million value for each painting."

Art, in this exchange, is a vehicle for market manipulation, a form of insider trading. Money for nothing. The value of Phelps's art, as she sees it, is inscribed on the art itself, art that illustrates what is done with money paid for art. Her work is both a rebuke of the art market and an acquiescence to that market. Because, as one dealer puts it, "there would be no drawing without the collector act of buying."

CAPITALISM

I ask the economist I meet in the bar if he can tell me what capitalism is. First he wants to know if I'm serious. Then he says there are a few different ways to answer that question. He'll start with the most generous: Capitalism is a way of thinking that made it possible for people to leave feudalism. The art historian next to us makes a sound of disgust and walks away. What? the economist smiles. I warned you that it was generous!

In terms of taxonomy, the economist says, capitalism describes one way goods and services can be exchanged. This mode of exchange is distinct from socialism, for instance. But an economy can be composed of various modes of exchange. Our economy in the United States isn't pure capitalism—we have a lot of socialism mixed in. We have free schools, free roads, free health care for the elderly and the very poor. In a purely capitalist economy, he says, none of us would be breathing this air—he gestures toward the dim hallway of the bar—without paying for it.

"We are all communists with our closest friends," David Graeber writes, "and feudal lords when dealing with small children." We move between different systems of moral accounting, he writes, but all social systems, including capitalism, rest on a bedrock of everyday communism. By everyday communism he means the principle: "From each according to their abilities, to each according to their needs." An entire economy couldn't be organized this way, Graeber argues, but many of our daily interactions already are. This is how we exchange information, for instance, in conversation.

Now the economist and Vojislav are talking about the communism of their youth in the former Yugoslavia. That was socialism, not communism, Vojislav clarifies for me. It was only called communism from the outside, not from the inside. Communism was an ideal, to be achieved in the far future, hopefully. People thought communism was a good idea, the economist points out, but nobody imagined that capitalism was going to make our lives better.

The peasants who rebelled against feudalism in the fourteenth century weren't imagining capitalism. They were imagining an end to forced labor. Later, as feudalism gave way to capitalism and common land was made into private property, the common people rebelled again and again, over hundreds of years, tearing down fences and digging up the hedges that enclosed private land.

During the English Revolution of the 1640s, when the king was executed, there was an upwelling of resistance to all sorts of authority, including the authority of the propertied class. "There were, we may oversimplify, two revolutions in mid-seventeenth-century England," Christopher Hill writes. "The one which succeeded established the sacred rights of property . . . gave political power to the propertied . . . and removed all impediments to the triumph of the ideology of the men of property—the protestant ethic."

That revolution, the one that succeeded, was a capitalist revolution. The other revolution, the one that did not succeed, was led by shepherds, tinkers, soldiers, and itinerant preachers. They were mostly unarmed, as only the propertied class was allowed to carry weapons. They rebelled with words, in a proliferation of pamphlets, and with acts of defiance, like refusing to remove their hats for their superiors and planting vegetables on land they didn't own.

Capitalism didn't just naturally evolve out of feudalism, as if it were a higher form of life, Silvia Federici argues. And it wasn't a revolution. "Capitalism was the response of the feudal lords, the patrician merchants, the bishops and popes, to a centuries-long social conflict that, in the end, shook their power." Capitalism, she writes, was a counterrevolution.

Among the rebels who resisted that counterrevolution were the Diggers, who called themselves the True Levellers. They imagined a new economy, in which people would work with each other, rather than for each other. They were not just ahead of their time, Hill notes, they were ahead of ours.

They fled to America, the radicals of that time, where their ideas have been forgotten. This country was not only colonized by slave owners, in the interests of property, it was also colonized by dissenters, whose descendants were abolitionists. "Our heavily redacted history has meant the loss of many options," writes Marilynne Robinson. One of those options being a society that understands itself as valuing people above capital.

WHITE RUSSIANS

Ivana wants to see the exhibit of early Soviet art, but by the time we get to it our children are restless, standing too close to paintings, careening toward plinths, and chasing each other around corners.

Last night, John and I paid a babysitter $40 so that we could go see *I Am Not Your Negro*. The theater had a bar and we ordered two White Russians. When the bartender asked what movie we were seeing, John said the one about Baldwin. I asked him why he didn't name the title of the film. It just felt like too much, John said, to order two White Russians for two white Americans and then top it off by saying I am not your negro.

The Whites, in Russia, were opposed to the Reds, the communists. Beyond that, they didn't have a common ideology. They were bourgeois liberals and traditional monarchists and orthodox Christians. They were from the Left and the Right, they were patriotic and suspicious of politics. They were Whites only because they weren't Reds.

I pause in front of El Lissitzky's *Beat the Whites with the Red Wedge*, a poster of a red triangle piercing a white circle. It looks so modern, so contemporary, Ivana says. Those stark geometric shapes, radical at the time, are now the language of corporate logos. It's a reminder that revolution needs to be constantly remade, reimagined. Maintained. Ivana translates the text of another poster for me: "The enemy never sleeps." She grew up with slogans like this, she says, the enemy within.

A speech by Lenin is playing from a loudspeaker while his words scroll across a screen in front of us. He's saying things like: We must stop the spread of global capitalism before all the wealth of the world is held by a very few. That seems reasonable, Ivana remarks wryly. But now that all the wealth of the world is held by a very few, it is no longer a revolutionary sentiment. It's just an artifact in a museum.

Our children are whispering to each other and laughing quietly. We're ignoring them, but I overhear enough of their whispering to gather that they're imagining all the damage they want to do to the museum. J is describing how he will swing from a hanging light fixture to crash into a painting and then drop to the floor and kick over a sculpture. They are planning a revolt against museums, against boredom, against being kept quiet, against being told what's important. I'm in favor of their revolt, in spirit, but I intend to suppress it. There will be no revolution on my watch.

SPIES

Have you seen what a declassified FBI file looks like these days? my brother asks. He teaches history and has just finished writing his dissertation. There are no thick black lines anymore, he says. Now an empty white box covers the page that has been redacted—it's a blank. And there's a code that designates the reason for the blank. Most often, the code is 5 U.S.C. § 552 (b)(1): national security.

I don't know what it means, I tell him. Russians keep appearing in this book I'm writing, and spies, and the FBI. It's a metaphor, I know that much. I can't quite decipher the code, but it has something to do with security. The spies are artists, I think, or anyone who lives inside a value system that isn't their own. Artists can't be expected to remain loyal to a regime that has made their work worthless. Maybe this is what Alexander Chee means when he suggests that all writers are class traitors, "no matter their social class." I want to be a class traitor, but I suspect that I'm more attracted to the romance of treason than the reality.

You should read *The Captive Mind* by Czesław Miłosz, my brother suggests. Miłosz, a poet, lived through the Nazi occupation of Warsaw and the Soviet Union's postwar invasion of Poland. Miłosz didn't want to leave the place where the language of his poetry was spoken. "Language," he wrote, "is the only homeland." And so he remained in Poland, full of ambivalence. He refused the Cold War dictate that you must either love communism or love the United States, my brother says. He hated both. He didn't want to live in a totalitarian state and he didn't want to live in consumer capitalism. Both, he knew, were bad for artists.

Miłosz believed that the revolution had the highest goal on earth, which was to end "man's exploitation of man." But he never joined the party. He despised the practices of the Communist government, the repression and the violence, though he worked as a diplomat for that government in the years before he went into exile.

Ketman, my brother says, is the word Miłosz used for living undercover, in secret opposition to the regime that wrote his paycheck. He borrowed the concept from Islamic theology, which allowed true believers to conceal their faith when surrounded by unbelievers. For Miłosz, ketman was something like the art of passing. "To say something is white when one thinks it black," he wrote, "to smile inwardly when one is outwardly solemn, to hate when one manifests love, to know when one pretends not to know, and thus to play one's adversary for a fool (even as he is playing you for one)." That is the game of ketman.

"It is a way of living with contradiction," Jacob Mikanowski writes. "It allows those adept at it to create private sanctuaries of the mind, untouched by compromise, even as compromise floods the rest of their lives."

"Stalin's Man in the Black Press" is the chapter of my brother's dissertation that I keep returning to. It tells the history of Homer Smith, an African American journalist who left the United States for Russia in 1932, hoping to escape discrimination. His work as the Moscow correspondent for the Associated Negro Press attracted the attention of the FBI, which was investigating subversion in the black press. The stories published by the black press, stories of Americans educated at Tuskegee and Howard who went to Russia for the opportunity to work as scientists and engineers, were undermining the official story the government wanted told. Smith reported back to the United States that in a crowded Moscow bus two Soviets had stood to allow him a seat, and in the public bath of a provincial village a Russian boy had scrubbed his back.

Smith married a Ukrainian woman and took an official post writing propaganda for the Communist Party. He wasn't just passing, he'd been taken with communism since before he left the States, and he willfully produced sentences like "Shaban

Abash and hundreds of thousands of other Abkhazians, now liberated, love Stalin as their closest and best teacher and truest leader." But he never joined the party.

A friend of Smith's, another African American communist, was among the million who were sent to prison camps during the Great Purge of 1936, and his wife's sister was among the thousands who disappeared. All foreigners were suspect in the paranoia that followed the purges, and Smith's blackness marked him as a foreigner. He became a Soviet citizen, but that didn't make him any less foreign.

Smith was accused of being "infected by his own peculiar Negro nationalism." This, from another African American communist. He survived that accusation, and he survived World War II, serving as a war correspondent for the Associated Press. But he wanted to make another escape. When he tried to regain his US citizenship after fourteen years in Russia, the FBI considered him too much of a security risk. What made him suspect was not his communist sympathies but, as his heavily redacted FBI file reveals, his "protests against alleged racial discrimination and inequality in America." That was the threat to national security.

Smith left Russia for Ethiopia and renounced his Soviet citizenship, but he was never allowed to reclaim his US citizenship. He became a stateless person. Or he had always been a stateless person, in possession of a precarious citizenship, as conditional and prone to repeal as ever. He was an American, but he had no country. "The romance of treason never occurred to us for the brutally simple reason that you can't betray a country you don't have," James Baldwin writes. You can't be a traitor if you've never been a citizen.

CITIZENS

I'm sitting on the floor of the library, between two shelves, holding *The World Falls Away* in my lap while I read *The Communist Manifesto* on my phone. The text is tiny and I can just barely make it out. The lives of workers, I discern, are becoming more precarious. And the bourgeoisie is producing "its own grave-diggers."

I've just come from a meeting with my boss's boss, who explained to me that artists don't want secure jobs. They prefer flexibility, he said. Why can't they have both? I wondered. He detailed his plan to hire more artists into part-time positions with limited contracts. The longer he talked, the more his reasoning sounded like the justification for Uber's business model.

Precarious was Merriam-Webster's word of the day recently. This is how I learned that "depending on the will or pleasure of another" was the original meaning of *precarious*, and that it comes from the Latin for *prayer*. Precarity is everywhere, it seems. Maybe it is, as Anna Lowenhaupt Tsing writes, "the condition of our time." It is also the defining feature of an entire class of people, the precariat.

"Everybody, actually" is the economist Guy Standing's answer to his own question, "Who enters the precariat?" By everybody, he means potentially anybody. Illness or disability can force somebody into the precariat, as can divorce, war, or natural disaster. The precariat is composed of migrant workers and temp workers and contract workers and part-time workers. People who work unstable jobs that offer "no sense of career." There are few opportunities to advance in these jobs, and no way to bargain for better terms. Some of the precariat are not citizens of the countries where they work. Others are citizens on paper, officially equal to other citizens, but lacking, in practice, equal protection under the law, or an equal ability to vote, or equal access to health care.

They are not really citizens, Standing suggests, but denizens. In ancient Rome, denizens were granted the right to work, but not the right to participate in political life. In medieval Europe, denizens were resident aliens, granted some but not all of the rights of native citizens. And the word *denizens*, Standing notes, "was also used to refer to non-slave blacks in the United States before the abolition of slavery."

The precariat is not easily recognizable as a class, even to itself. It includes convicts and asylum seekers and single mothers and artists. It includes educated people who can't find the work for which they were educated. And people without college degrees who can't find the kinds of jobs their parents and grandparents worked, in factories and coal mines. What they all have in common is a lack of security.

The precariat is not what we used to call the working class, Standing clarifies. Those workers held long-term jobs with fixed hours. They had unions and pensions, and they knew their employers. Uber drivers don't know their employers or their fellow employees. They lack, among other forms of security, the security of working with people they know, and people who know them.

The Uber drivers who take me to the airport are recent immigrants who are driving until they find other work or musicians who are driving while they're not on tour or retired utilities workers who are driving to pay their health care expenses or, sometimes, people who are driving because they don't want a regular job with regular demands and a regular schedule.

Some people choose their precarity—evidence that precarity is not just a condition of our time, but a response to it. The precariat includes people who have forgone stable employment and retirement savings for temp work and travel and an uncertain future. Their very existence is unsettling, suggesting, as it does, that there might be something worth more than security.

WATER

We're driving through the mountains of France talking about affluence. Looking at the map this morning, John noticed that *affluence* is the French word for the tributaries of a river. He wonders if the word once suggested a great river of wealth flowing into smaller affluences. Was it comforting for people to think of money replenishing itself in a regenerative cycle with the rains? Along with affluence, there are liquid assets, and trickle-down economics, and the rising tides that float all boats. Why is water so often a metaphor for money? Perhaps because we like to believe that our economic system is naturally occurring, not man-made. Maybe the movement of money feels inevitable if you imagine it as water, with only blameless gravity participating in the accumulation of wealth.

Now we're talking about *flow*—the way these mountain roads must be driven, without knowing what's ahead, around blind curves, through single-lane tunnels, past rock faces pitching into the road. In Pont-en-Royans the stone bridge is still warm from the sun as I lean over it looking down into a gorge full of shadows. The river is far below and so are slick stairs and a walkway cut into the rock and abandoned long ago. I watch trout in the shallows and remember swimming in the waterfall earlier today. The air was full of honeysuckle and there were fat, tattooed French wading in the cold water and a family of North Africans picnicking on the muddy bank. The spray was like little stones on my face as I swam toward the waterfall, and I could feel the incredible power of it, the energy churning under the surface.

This village has a museum called Musée de l'Eau, the Museum of Water, but I don't go in. I already feel like I'm in a museum of water. "Nothing is more useful than water," Adam Smith wrote in 1776, "but it will purchase scarce any thing; scarce any thing can be had in exchange for it." Diamonds are useless, he added, but they can be exchanged for many things. He didn't foresee a time when wars would be fought over water as often as diamonds, but he could already see that the things that meet our most urgent needs are often worthless.

ART

I'm standing outside the Louvre wondering about the cost. Not of the palaces, but of my pleasures. There were armed soldiers marching across the Tuileries this morning, and soldiers striding slowly down the Champ de Mars. In Montmartre last night I saw them climbing the stairs by Sacré-Cœur, two abreast, with machine guns.

Inside, past the black men selling tiny Eiffel Towers, I stand in front of the painting of the coronation of Napoleon. His wife is receiving her crown, and this is where Beyoncé will dance with a phalanx of women, every shade of brown. *I can't believe we made it,* she'll sing, meaning her marriage and her money. And her people, too. "African-American capitalism isn't much different from any other kind," K. Leander Williams will write of her, "but it can often signal that something astonishing is at work." Generations into the future, Beyoncé's grandchildren and their children's children, as yet unborn, will all be rich. *That's a lot of brown children on your* Forbes *list,* she sings. Her wealth is a grand redemption of a debt long unpaid. But it is not an untroubled triumph. *Pay me in equity, pay me in equity*, Beyoncé sings. Money is no substitute, really, for equity. And to be coronated queen under capitalism is to claim a domain that comes, as Marx put it, "dripping from head to toe, from every pore, with blood and dirt."

I pause in front of *The Raft of the Medusa*, where the bodies of the drowned men are held by the survivors. *The Medusa* wrecked off the coast of Africa, on its way to colonize Senegal. A young man is splayed across the raft naked, his flesh glowing with otherworldly light. I gaze at his midriff, so tenderly rendered. Géricault studied cadavers for this work, and then painted from live models, one of whom was the young Delacroix, also a painter.

And here is *The Massacre at Chios* by Delacroix, which is subtitled *A Greek Family Awaiting Death or Slavery*. It's a grim scene, but beautiful, the bodies of the hostages lean and muscled, pale breasts bared. "Its political gesture was important," John Berger writes of this painting. "But it remains a gesture. It has nothing to do with any true imaginative understanding of either death or slavery. It is a voluptuous charade. The woman tied to the horse is a languorous sex-offering, the rope round her arm like an exotic snake playing with her."

This is the erotics of ownership. And it holds heat, even as that rope chafes. I doubt that I have ever achieved any true imaginative understanding of death or slavery, or that I will, before I die. But I still believe that death and slavery are tied up in the same rope that binds that woman.

The Venus de Milo is around the corner, and I lead J to the front of the crowd but he can't see anything because so many arms are stretched out above his head taking pictures. What these crowds have done to the works of art they came to see, Berger writes, is acquire them. "Or, rather, they have acquired the right to refer to them in a proprietary context." Art, he insists, can't escape being property.

I feel for the art. But I take pleasure in it, too. "A love of art has been a useful concept to the European ruling classes for over a century and a half," Berger writes. "The love was said to be their own. With it they could claim kinship with the civilizations of the past and the possession of those moral virtues associated with 'beauty.'"

All this is true, I know. And then I look up at the ceiling, where bodies float through the sky in flowing robes, celestial and corporeal. I don't want to own any of this, or claim it as mine, but I want to touch it—I want to get close enough to see the vein on the flank of the marble centaur, the vein that seems to be alive and pumping blood.

BLOOD

I'm brought, along with six other writers, to a house composed entirely of echoing ballrooms. We've been asked to explain to the people gathered here, all of them wealthy, why they should give money to an artists' community. We walk through a room with crystal chandeliers and a room with a tapestry into a room full of paintings of water hung in gilt frames all the way to the ceiling, as in the Louvre.

The artists' community is a place where artists can work on their art while living, temporarily, like the wealthy. A groundskeeper tends the lawn and gardens, a housekeeper vacuums the floors and changes the sheets once a week, and a cook makes dinner every night. Over the course of each year, more than a hundred artists share an estate that once belonged to one family. In return for appearing at this fundraiser I will be granted a three-week stay at this estate, where I will discover how little time it takes to acquire the mindset of entitlement. The first time the housekeeper knocks on my door to change my sheets, I will feel grateful for the luxury, but the second time, I will be annoyed by the interruption.

At first, I don't understand why we need to explain that artists must have time and space to make their art and that this costs money. As champagne is passed around, some conversation clarifies this. The people here believe that if artists are successful then their success should produce all the money they need. And if they aren't successful then they don't deserve money.

This is followed by a dinner in a mansion, which I hear the host describing, when I come in the door, as modest. Why is gang violence such a problem in Chicago, my dinner companions are wondering as I sit down at the long banquet table. Someone says something about bad families.

At the suggestion of my host, I move to the other end of the table, where a man mentions that I might be interested in an essay titled "The Tragedy of the Commons." I've just read that essay, I tell him, yesterday. He hesitates and then explains it to me. The tragedy, he says, is that everyone will always take as much as they can from the commons. This isn't my sense of the tragedy—the tragedy is that by the time that essay was written the commons had already been lost and the regulations that once prevented everyone from taking as much as they could from the commons had been forgotten. But the idea that the commons cannot be regulated, I know, is the interpretation of that essay favored by free-market capitalists. And that's what has made it so enduring, despite the fact that it was written as an argument for limiting the "breeding" of the poor and is riddled with inaccuracies and outright false-hoods. Its veracity is less important than its influence, one of my colleagues once said of that essay. Meaning, the lies we want to believe tell us something about ourselves.

I excuse myself to join a group of women gathered by the dessert table. One of them tells me that she invests in medical technology. Investment, I'm reminded, is a line of work for the wealthy. I still have "The Tragedy of the Commons" on my mind. I tell her about the work I do in the garden at the elementary school. As I weed and water there, I say, I watch other women coming and going from their volunteer work inside. They do homework with the children who come in early for the free breakfast and they run a book exchange and they give talks about art and they share the work of supporting the school. I'm grateful, I tell her, that these women value work that doesn't pay—someone has to care. But it still bothers me to see only women doing unpaid work. It reminds me of the word Ivana translated for me as "mandatory volunteer work."

Capital, the investor tells me, is something women didn't have until recently. We couldn't even carry our own credit cards until 1974, she reminds me. We didn't amass capital, we didn't understand it, and we didn't learn how to manage it. We didn't have mothers and grandmothers teaching us about capital. But here's the thing—she circles her womb with her hand—we are capital. We are the means of production. I had three children, she says. I've been the means of production. Now I want to own the means of production.

I pause over this, wondering what it means to own yourself. And wondering if the very idea of owning yourself requires, as she suggests, imagining your body as capital. Now she's saying, You know, money isn't bad. Money isn't the problem. Money is the stuff that flows through the problem. Money is the blood, she says. You can test blood to find out what the problem is, but the presence of blood alone isn't going to diagnose the problem.

As she says this, I look around and see it everywhere. The plush furniture splashed in blood, the catered table sopping with blood, the manicured garden watered with blood.

BICYCLE MANIFESTO

Blood is seeping through a gauze bandage on my foot and pooling in my sneaker as I sit in the last row of folding chairs at the center of a ballroom listening to the artist Cauleen Smith talk about her *Bicycle Manifesto*. Black people on bikes, she says, are everywhere and nowhere. "When you look at bicycle magazines we're not on the covers, we're not in the magazines," she says. "And yet in any city, there are black people riding bikes everywhere, with a particular kind of style and a particular kind of purpose."

A parade of style and purpose passes my window every day. Boys swerve by giddily, helmetless, in groups of two or three. A woman tows something heavy in a trailer behind her bicycle. Teenagers text as they ride home from school, loose-limbed, one with their machines. And then there's the man who rides handless, dancing, with neon wheel lights, carrying, as he passes, his own bubble of music with him, a small radius of joy.

"When I started riding a bike I realized there's a real relationship between a body powering itself going down the street and the way you interact with your community," Smith says. "The violence of the power of a car is an alienating device. It's the last thing we need in our neighborhoods."

Cars are like armor, Rachel Cusk observes. They are designed to protect the people inside them, not anyone else. The people outside cars must always be wary of cars, must drive them, in fact, with their minds. Even people who don't know how to drive know how to gauge the momentum of a car, know how long it will take to stop, and know that it should be treated as if it's not just huge and heavy, but also blind.

I was once hit twice by the same car, which clipped my front wheel as it turned into a parking spot and then quickly reversed to straighten out and hit my wheel again just as I righted my bike. The driver saw me the second time, put down her cell phone, and yelled at me for not having a light on my bike, though it wasn't dark and her headlights weren't on.

Bicycles have the same rights and duties as motor vehicles. But being governed by the same laws doesn't produce equality. A bicycle doesn't occupy a full lane, is rarely granted the three-foot passing margin required by law, and must use signals that not everyone understands. Bicycles belong to a different class and they can't expect to be treated like cars. And so, bicycles break the rules, riding through stop signs and red lights. Like the people who occupy neighborhoods that are overpoliced and underprotected, bicycles know that what keeps them safe on the street is not the law, but their own vigilance, quickness, and wit.

A bicycle in traffic must be predictive to the point of clairvoyance, must know the cars better than the cars know themselves, must understand their motivations and their common blunders. Cars don't always signal their intentions. And cars aren't always nice to each other, though they usually show each other some respect in deference to the damage they can do to each other. They are like important men in conversation with other important men. Bicycles are sometimes kindly accommodated by cars, often ignored, occasionally respected, sometimes nervously followed, and frequently not even seen. In this sense, riding in traffic is not unlike being a woman among men.

You're taking up the whole road, a woman in a large SUV once yelled out her window at John, who was riding his bike along the shoulder. Cars make you stupid, in the way wealth makes you stupid. In the way any sort of power makes you stupid, really. And it is this, my own stupidity, that I dislike most about driving.

On a bicycle, I'm alert, aware of everything. It's exhilarating, the narrow margin, the exposure to injury, the steadying force of the spinning wheels. And then, for the sake of comfort or convenience, I get into a car. The sound of the street is dulled. I sit back and turn on the radio. I become distracted. Speed is easy, unearned, and bicycles are now an annoyance. I forget who I was just moments ago.

When I was young in New York I used to lie awake at night as my commute played back before my eyes—the truck full of lumber that turned in front of me, the policeman who threatened to write me a ticket after he opened his door into my lane and sent me over my handlebars, the city bus that bore down on me as I struggled to unwind my shoelace from my derailleur. I now ride in a protected bike lane nearly all the time. And I own a bicycle that cost as much as the first car I ever bought, a used Geo Metro that I got for $2,000, a purchase that made me proud.

The car is a symbol of maturity for the average black person, Smith acknowledges. And for the average American, too, I think. But she wants us "to consider the toy, the bicycle, as an actual device of liberation."

Yes, I think, in delight, writing down everything she says. My foot is stretched out in front of me bleeding because of a fall from my bicycle. This fall was entirely my fault—I ran straight into a post after having too much to drink. There was no traffic, no car to blame. But if I had been in a car I would have hurt the post, rather than myself.

Precarity is not the price of riding a bicycle, I think, so much as what it has to offer. Wind, a rush of blood, fissures and pits in the asphalt, an errant animal, eyes in a mirror, glint of sunlight on chrome, scent of lake water, catcalls, a soaring feeling. But that is not to say that liberation doesn't have a price.

THE HUG

I'm at work, meeting with a student who is writing a story without a plot. It's about a woman who doesn't do much of anything. She doesn't work a job and she rarely speaks. She considers visiting her mother but then she doesn't. She's afraid to drive. She moves through her day quietly observing the things around her—milk in a bowl, dust on a rag, the broken head of a doll that used to be her plaything.

We begin by discussing books with no setting beyond the writer's mind, like *This Is Not a Novel* and *Dictée*. And then plotless books, like *Pond* and *Holy Land*. And books with a narrator who speaks very little, like *Outline* and *Agaat*. I recognize this student's ambition, but I have some questions. I want to know why this woman, her character, is avoiding the world beyond her home. And how she affords to live in a house without a job. I have a more difficult question for this student, too, a question that I wouldn't have been able to answer at her age. Why is she rejecting the expectations of her genre—why does she want to write a story that's not a story?

I'm circling this question carefully, preparing to ask it, when my desk phone rings.

It's my boss, asking if I can come up to the office of the man I call Reply All. When I arrive, she suggests that I hug Reply All. I hesitate. I've just told her, this morning, that he's domineering in meetings. He outranks me and won't let me forget it. Reply All has his arms spread wide, his head tilted. Come on, he says. Both my boss and her deputy are here looking on—administering this hug is a two-boss job. I submit to the hug and sit down in anger. The deputy boss says that what I recognized as domination is just the ordinary nature of a work relationship. This is like a marriage, she says, gesturing toward me and Reply All. No, I say, it's not. We should be careful, my boss cautions. But the deputy boss is already saying, Well, you *are* married to one of your colleagues. What this has to do with anything is beyond me, until I see what she's suggesting. I'm already a wife at work, so I shouldn't be surprised to be treated like a wife at work. I'm so furious now that I'm crying. I can barely talk. Reply All sighs heavily. I want out of this as much as he does. But before I leave, my boss suggests another hug.

You didn't have to do that, John says sadly. He's chopping garlic and I'm cooking pasta, with the smell of Reply All's cologne still clinging to my shirt. I know, I say. I'm angry with myself. John wonders what I was thinking. I was thinking about the form that I have to submit to my boss to buy back my time, the form that requires her signature. That's not in the contract, John says, you're not trading hugs for signatures. But I'm trading something that's not in the contract, I say. And I'm coming to understand what it is.

Reply All doesn't speak to me after the meeting. He avoids me entirely and skirts the walls when we're in the same room. He does this for months, until the next time he sees me standing next to my boss. Then he heads straight for me and holds out his arms for another hug.

RESIGNATION

"As long as I live under the capitalistic system, I expect to have my life influenced by the demands of moneyed people," William Faulkner wrote in his resignation from his job as postmaster. "But I will be damned if I propose to be at the beck and call of every itinerant scoundrel who has two cents to invest in a postage stamp."

His resignation had the ring of rebellion, but it was a sad surrender to the system. Faulkner was postmaster at the University of Mississippi, where he had dropped out of college. He was in his twenties then and a friend had gotten him the job. Faulkner was asked for his resignation after an inspector discovered that he was writing a book in the back of the post office while people waited out front. He was also throwing mail in the trash. Faulkner went on to work the night shift in the power plant at the university. There wasn't much work to do between midnight and 4:00 a.m., so he used an overturned wheelbarrow as a desk. And that's where he wrote *As I Lay Dying*.

I was fired from a job once, in my twenties. The job was wait-ressing in an Italian restaurant on Madison Avenue. All the other waiters were men, so I knew I was out of my league. I had never waitressed, but I told the manager that I had worked in a diner one summer. That seemed somewhere between the truth and what he wanted to hear. He looked at me closely and asked where my people came from. Poland, I said, which was partly true. He was Polish too, and he wanted to know what my father, who he assumed was an immigrant, did for a living. My father, a doctor, was born in upstate New York, where his Polish grandparents were farmers. He was a farmer, I lied. What kind of farmer? I thought of the woods around my father's house, woods where mushrooms grew on rot-ting logs. I was the daughter of a Polish mushroom farmer. Could I speak any Polish? Just one phrase, which my grand-mother had often spoken to me as a child: Kiss me, I'm beg-ging you.

That got me the job, but I was not a good waitress. By the third day I had already been demoted to taking drink orders and serving coffee. By the fourth day, only coffee. On the fifth day, I caused an accident with the espresso machine and spilled coffee all over the manager's white shirt. The chef handed me a $20 bill, because in New York waitresses don't earn anything for their first week of work. He didn't want to see me sent away with nothing.

I was fired, but the manager still felt responsible for me. He couldn't put a poor farmer's daughter out on the street. So he brought me to the Museum of Modern Art. He knew some-one at the restaurant there who would hire me as a hostess, which he assured me required nothing more than a pretty face.

Several higher-ranking hostesses at the restaurant were not happy about my hire. They huddled together while I stood to the side, studying the seating chart. After a week or two, the top hostess came over to discuss the problem with me. I needed to wear some makeup, lipstick at least. And I had to shave my legs. They had standards, she said. My other choice was to be sent downstairs, where I would sit behind the infor-mation desk.

The job downstairs paid $5.15 per hour and it didn't come with one free meal per shift like the job upstairs. But I didn't mind because I could spend most of my time reading. And what I read at the information desk, having been demoted to doing what I really wanted to do, was *As I Lay Dying*.

WORK

She works hard for the money, I sing to John, who is naked, just out of the shower. She's surprisingly convincing as a waitress, he says. He's thinking of the photo of Donna Summer on the album cover, dressed as a waitress in a diner with her pencil poised, ready to take an order. Maybe she was a waitress, I say. He doubts that. She had already released her first single by the time she was twenty.

In the music video she's not a waitress but a witness, a born-again disco queen union rep for working women. The video begins with a white woman waking from a dream of dancing to go to work cleaning floors, then waiting tables, then operating a sewing machine. And there's Summer, on the other side of the sweatshop, toying with the woman's time card, singing, *You better treat her right.* When the woman looks out her kitchen window while cooking for her children, there's Summer, leaning against the house next door. Summer isn't there when a man grabs the woman's butt while she waits tables, but when she falls in the restaurant there's Summer, helping her up.

Summer was having her own work trouble when she wrote that song. She wanted to be released from her record label but litigation had determined that she owed them one more album. "She Works Hard for the Money" was the title song of her eleventh album, the album she was contractually obligated to make. The song wasn't written about a waitress, but about a bathroom attendant. Her name was Onetta Johnson, and Summer found her sleeping in the bathroom of a Los Angeles restaurant where she gave out hand towels for tips. She was exhausted, she told Summer, because she worked another job during the day.

With a nod to "Thriller," the final scene of the music video features women leaving work, like zombies rising from graves, and gathering in the street to dance in formation. There's a police officer and a postal worker and a doctor and a prostitute and a construction worker and a chef and maybe even an archeologist, all dancing with the waitress who wanted to be a dancer.

Why are you singing Donna Summer? John wants to know. I've got work on my mind. I've been weighing what I'll gain and lose if I quit my job. I'll lose my students and my library privileges. I'll gain time to write but I'll have to write for money. And if I sell a book, I'll be contractually obligated to make art. Don't do anything, John says, that will take the pleasure out of your work.

ALL I WANTED

David and I are talking about Barbie, Nazis, and Emily Dickinson. He tells me that a neighbor of the Dickinsons once remarked that time must move slowly for Emily, who had so much time to herself. This was repeated to Emily, who responded with a quote from Robert Browning, *Time, why, Time was all I wanted!*

I'm certain that her life was not unhappy, I tell David, but my only evidence is her work. All those exclamation points! Yes, she didn't publish. But publication is not where the pleasure is in writing. David responds with a quote from Dickinson, *How public – like a Frog.*

What the Nazis did, David says, hoarding art for its monetary value, is like what the art market is doing now. I just read an article, I say, about Martin Shkreli, who bought the rights to a Wu-Tang Clan album that nobody has ever heard. Now the feds have the album, because Shkreli was convicted of defrauding investors. He also inflated the price of a drug used by AIDS patients by 5,500 percent, but that wasn't a crime.

The Wu-Tang Clan didn't intend to entangle themselves with a free-market capitalist who pushed the profit margin on medicine, but they did want to make a high-end collector's item. Their album, printed in only one copy and encased in a silver box, was an attempt to restore cash value to music that streams for free. Music is not easily commodified in our time. Music, RZA complains, "doesn't receive the same treatment as art."

We walk to the grocery store, where David buys two chocolate bars for us and some bubbles for J. There are three different kinds of bubbles to choose from. Which one? David wonders. Maybe one of each? See, he reminds me, he likes commodities. He's a collector, after all, back to Barbie for the third time. He thinks this time he can finish, by finally giving himself what he wants. He tells me about a memory from his boyhood of a small black vinyl trunk full of Barbie clothes, forbidden to him, and of his longing for that trunk. He has to have it, he tells me, and he has to take the Barbie clothes he has collected out of their acid-free paper and put them in that trunk, because he doesn't want to come back in another life to collect Barbie.

I think of David's poem: *Write me down as one / who loved poetry and the / paste jewels of pop art.* He asks if I collect anything. Maybe plants? He once saw me leave a party to buy a plant I'd been wanting from a nursery down the street. I do keep a list on my desk of my desires: cornelian cherry, red lake currant, scarlet prince peach. But the plants are not mine as soon as I put them in the ground. My garden isn't a collection. It's a place where I practice care, and where I take time. Time being, in the end, all I ever wanted.

CARE

I have come home to care for my mother, who just had sur-
gery. I help her change the bandage over her heart, but the
worst of her recovery is already over. She lies on a mattress on
the floor and assigns me tasks, all of them like the impossible
tasks from a fairy tale. She wants me to walk through a field
of thorns and find the lone pear tree growing there. She wants
me to organize a closet full of rusty saw blades and loose
feathers, and she wants me to fill a bucket with stones all of
the same size. She comes with me into the woods on my
search for stones and while I'm ruminating about the point-
lessness of this task she's alive to the world. She shows me a
maidenhair fern, the most beautiful of ferns she says. Back at
the house she looks very thin on her mattress, which she's
dragged outside now, but she's glowing in the evening sun.

I feel a rising aggravation with the work she has given me, and
shame over my aggravation. These tasks aren't difficult, just
hard to fathom. There is rarely profit from work in my mother's realm. It must be done for its own sake. My mother used

to work through many different grades of sandpaper, finer and finer, until the knot of wood that she had sawed off a dead tree was as soft as skin, and then she would oil it until it shone, the purpose of all this work being to reveal the beauty of the knot.

I wade through the field of wild raspberries, the thorns tearing at my clothes, and this task seems newly impossible. The pursuit of beauty is fruitless, I think. Care can be given but not taken, love can't be proven, and I won't ever find the pear tree. But then I find it, there among all the thorns, still alive, with just two branches and a few leaves. And I care for the tree, just as my mother instructed.

As I work, I remember the rest of the fairy tale, the one where the witch assigns the girl impossible tasks. A doll given to the girl by her mother whispers in the girl's ear, soothes her despair, and helps her complete the tasks. The girl's success vexes the witch, but she grants the girl power by giving her a skull full of flames. My mother, I know, would say that the evil witch and the good mother are the same woman.

ANCIENT MEW

In the final chore of a series of chores, J helps me cut down the hedge in front of our house and dig out the roots. We do this under the afternoon sun and a neighbor crosses the street to joke about child labor. J is dripping sweat and dirt, and I'm satisfied that he has earned his dollar, the last dollar he needs to buy the Pokémon card that he wants.

My stepmother is horrified when she learns that J has spent $7 on a single card when a pack of ten cards can be bought for $3. You let him waste his money like that? she asks me. It isn't really his money unless he can use it the way he wants, I explain. And making mistakes with money is one of the best ways to learn how not to make mistakes with money.

J is delighted with the card, which is called Ancient Mew. Unlike other cards, it does not have a number in the upper right-hand corner. Or, it does not have a decipherable number. It has a symbol that J claims is ancient Egyptian. Part of the allure of this card, I come to understand, is that how powerful it may or may not be, and thus how valuable, is open to interpretation.

Ancient Mew causes a stir on the playground, where boys are trading cards on the asphalt. One boy tells J that this card is very powerful and that he feels jealous. Another boy tells him that it isn't powerful at all and that he should give it away because it's worthless. Another boy says that J should give the card to him, because he has a card-copying machine at home and he can copy it and bring it back tomorrow. Another boy tells J that he should give the card to him because his entire collection was just stolen. J breaks down in tears. Then he runs off to the bushes at the far edge of the playground. When he returns he is happy again. He has given the card away to a four-year-old in the bushes who doesn't know anything about Pokémon.

THE GIFT

I run into Will on the path by the lake and he asks if I've read Winstanley. I don't know what he's talking about. Will is a friend from work, an early modernist who reads books from the seventeenth century. And now I remember. In 1649, Gerrard Winstanley led the Diggers in an act of protest, the digging and planting of a patch of vacant land outside London. Their plan was to give the food they grew to anyone who worked with them, and to forge a new economy—not feudalism and not capitalism either.

I started reading Winstanley's *The Law of Freedom*, I tell Will, but then I set it aside to read Lewis Hyde's *The Gift*. All that stuff about gift economies, Will says, strikes him as nostalgic. The gift exchanges Hyde writes of, the Kula of the Massim and the potlatch of the Kwakwaka'wakw, are from far away and long ago. But those exchanges serve as metaphors for the practice of art—the gift the artist is given by art and the gift the artist gives in making art—which happens in the here and now. And in the here and now, we can't seem to speak of anything, art or our own children, in terms that aren't drawn from capital investment.

Maybe from inside capitalism, Will says, every other system looks improbable and nostalgic, and every other way of life is hard to believe.

Maybe what makes me nostalgic for gift economies, I suggest, is all the time I spent among poets when I was young. It was poetry, Hyde writes, that brought him to writing, as it was for me, "and it was in the poetry world that I could see most clearly the disconnect between art and the common forms of earning a living." The poets I knew made their money like everyone else, as teachers or bartenders, but what they did for poetry, and for each other, was most often given away. They weren't trading for reputation or influence—none of us had any of that yet. But we had the pleasures of exchange.

The poets gave away their own books, handbound sometimes, and letterpress broadsides made on antiquated machinery, they gave their time to editing each other's work in their bedroom offices, they paid to have it printed, they carried each other's books in suitcases to give to other poets, they used their day jobs at copy shops to print chapbooks and zines, they performed their work for nothing but applause, and they gave each other places to stay, couches to sleep on. Not for profit, but for literature. I guess, I tell him, it's easy for me to believe there's an alternative to capitalism because I feel like I've lived it. Within capitalism, of course.

Now I'm back on the path alone, walking past the beach where sailboats are stored on the sand with their masts up, waiting to be sailed. I hear piano music over the shushing of the waves, and then I see a piano on the sand between two boats. It's an upright, like ours, just slightly more ragged, and I can't imagine how it got so far out onto the beach—a truck and ramps must have been involved, but there's no evidence of that now. A man is sitting at the piano, shirtless under the sun, playing a song that might be a show tune. There's a blue tarp crumpled around his feet and I wonder if this piano has been there all summer, weathering storms quietly, without my ever noticing. The lines on the masts of the sailboats are clinking in the wind, keeping their own time. The man has his back to the path and is facing the water. He's playing for the lake.

CONSUMPTION

The sound of a piano playing in the dark woke a guest staying in Emily Dickinson's house. "I can improvise better at night," she explained at breakfast. I'm Emily today, deep in her biography, breathing her air. David gave me this book, his copy, and when I saw the title, *My Wars Are Laid Away in Books*, I thought, yes, mine too. My pencil marks are on the pages now with David's pen. On one page he has underlined "a creator ex nihilo" and written "out of nothing."

John is using a blowtorch to light a fire in our fireplace. Matches take too much time. The blowtorch makes a light roar, the sound of evenly controlled gas exploding into flame as it's released from pressure. When the wood has caught and the flames are high against the brick, he sets the blowtorch on the mantel. It remains there, wrong and at the ready.

California is about to catch fire. I'll see it from an airplane, an airplane that will fuel future wildfires. Newspaper after newspaper will report that a place called Paradise has been destroyed, almost entirely consumed. South of Paradise, in Los Angeles, the rich will hire private firefighters to save their homes. The future, long predicted, has arrived. My son will inherit this future, along with this property, paid off in thirty years.

I don't know how to end this book, I tell Robyn. There's no end, there's no resolution. No, of course there isn't, she says. The only way to end it would be to burn your house down.

I laugh until I cough and then I can't stop coughing. I've caught consumption from Emily's biography, I think. Everyone was coming down with consumption back then and there was no cure. One of her neighbors drowned in her own blood. It was the leading cause of death, consumption. Even now, one fourth of the world's population is infected. More than a million people will die of consumption this year. Just not here.

"Readers put off by Emily Dickinson's class privileges," Alfred Habegger writes, "should not forget that she was far more exposed to pain and disease than most of us." I pause over this. Is he suggesting that our discomfort with wealth, political as it might be, should be eased by remembering that the wealthy also suffer? Or is he reminding us that we, of the presumed middle class, are now living lives more comfortable than hers? Perhaps he just wants us to recall that rich and poor alike died of consumption.

Health is a mark of money in our time, when a longer life span can be bought. The rich of this country are living to be older and older now, while everyone else is dying younger. "Perhaps the starkest measure of the failure of our economic policies," Binyamin Appelbaum writes, "is that the average American's life expectancy is in decline, as inequalities of wealth have become inequalities of health." Meanwhile, life remains the ultimate privilege, the living lording over the dead.

The servant who cooked and cleaned for the Dickinsons for thirty years, Margaret Maher, was paid $3 a week. Emily treated her with affection, but also talked down to her. Emily wasn't democratic, as Habegger puts it. But he won't have her written off: "Those who see nothing but class privilege should keep in mind that she was a noncitizen by force of custom and law, that many doors were closed to her, and that she left behind more good hard work than any of us."

Speaking of privilege, David said when he gave me her biography, it is a privilege to spend your life writing. Not a luxury, he clarified, but a privilege.

"I have no other Playmate," she said of her writing. She wrote in secret, stealing time for her work. Time not spent skimming the milk in the pantry or kneading bread in the kitchen. A fragment of a late-life letter to a man she loved but refused to marry, scissored away from whatever else it might have said, reads, "Don't you know that 'No' is the wildest word we consign to Language?"

THE HOLE

I spend most of my fortieth birthday digging a hole in my yard. It's six feet across, big enough to attract comments from neighbors and gather water from thunderstorms.

Sara gives me *The Unquiet Grave*, the book Cyril Connolly wrote the year he turned forty, when he was struggling with the question of what he wanted out of life. I can give this to you, Sara says, laughing, because you're not unhappy with your work. She means my writing. "Approaching forty, sense of total failure," Connolly writes. He has spent his life on comforts, traveling and running up debts. He likes soft cheeses and warm baths, but he fears that he is losing himself to pleasure. He sloshes with alcohol, as he puts it, and his mind has become "a worn gramophone record."

Pleasure is not necessarily harmful, he writes. But it "outrages that part of us which is concerned with growth." He wants to be more than he is. He is stagnating in his gin and whiskey, and in his memories of long afternoons in Paris. He wants to write a great work. He thinks he might have to give up his pleasures and suffer like the writers he admires. But he's not entirely convinced, as among his pleasures is the pleasure of writing: "O sacred solitary empty mornings, tranquil meditations—fruit of book-case and clock-tick, of note-book and arm-chair; golden and rewarding silence, influence of sun-dappled plane-trees, far-off noises of birds and horses, possession beyond price of a few cubic feet of air and some hours of leisure."

In my mind I call the hole my unquiet grave. As in, my unquiet grave is almost complete. And my unquiet grave needs only to be made a bit deeper now. I dug a hole like this last year, too, and in between these two holes I've determined that my job—not the work itself, but the weather around the work—is killing the pleasure I take in work.

The justification for this hole is a tree, its ball of roots bound in burlap, now leaning at an angle on my lawn. The man who sold me the tree said, Tell your guy when he plants this—and I cut him off to say that I was my guy, and that I was going to plant this tree myself. He sized me up and said, You don't want to do that. I've already done it, I told him. A couple waiting for his help laughed nervously and suggested that perhaps I could plant their tree, too.

I'm not for hire, I said, I just dig for myself.

My digging is a private protest, work for pleasure. It blisters my hands and I enjoy it. "To live in a decadence need not make us despair," Connolly suggests, "it is but one technical problem the more which an artist has to solve." The technical problem being, in part, the temptation to justify decadence.

The tree stands behind me, leaning. As I dig, a single phrase repeats in my head: "Canted vertiginously over the tailrace." It's from Joan Didion's essay about Hoover Dam, where a man from the Bureau of Reclamation takes her deep into the machinery of the dam to see a turbine and then says, "Touch it." It's an essay about power, I once told my students, in all its valences. "One cannot serve both beauty and power," Connolly writes, quoting Flaubert: "Le pouvoir est essentiellement stupide." Power is essentially stupid.

The hole is so big now that I have to get into it to dig. My neighbor leans over the fence in her scrubs, home for lunch from her job at the hospital. She suggests that I go out for happy hour tonight to celebrate my birthday. My hole doesn't look like a celebration to her. She spent all of last summer tearing down her fence, digging out the huge slugs of concrete that held the posts, and rebuilding it all again herself.

Some of this she did in the rain, at night, wearing a head-lamp. She describes the cocktail she wants me to order in such detail that she seems to be drinking it with me in her mind. I'm touched, but I'm distracted. I keep thinking, I'm in the hole! I can smell the raw umber of the clay, and I can feel it on my hands drying and cracking as the blisters rise. My neighbor finishes happy hour, her gift to me, and leaves for work.

"Approaching forty," Connolly writes, "a singular dream in which I almost grasped the meaning and understood the nature of what it is that wastes in wasted time."

Time and money, this neighbor once said to me, that's how you know what matters to a person. She spends her time and money on music and theater, going to concerts and plays. She invests in the arts. I think people are what matter to me, but I spend my time on writing and my money on this house. As I dig, I come to a decision. I will sell a book—this book—to buy myself time. My time, already spent on writing, will pay for itself. Like Foucault's pendulum, swinging from a 220-foot wire, the heavy polished bob gliding back and forth silently, charting the movement of the earth on its axis, it will be unmotored, free, and perpetual. But something is always lost to friction. The pendulum slows and stops. And the books, I know, may never be balanced on this, my desire for time.

I regard the wheelbarrow full of fresh dirt resting above my unquiet grave. Now I'm in the hole I dug myself, I think with amusement. It feels like an accomplishment.

NOTES

ON THE TITLE:

The title for this work first appeared within some sentences of appreciation that I wrote for Robyn Schiff's 2016 book *A Woman of Property*: "This brilliant revelation of having and being had winds like a spiral staircase down from the nursery, into the garden, through violence and lust and contagion, to the Greek tragedy that is the foundation on which our American tragedy is built. 'Every time I descend the stairs,' Schiff writes, 'I trespass what I already own.'"

A Woman of Property was written after Schiff bought her first house. *Having and Being Had* was written after I bought my first house, in response to Schiff's work and in conversation with Schiff herself. The title is an acknowledgment of our close collaboration and our shared trespasses.

ON THE COMFORTS:

I began keeping a new kind of diary shortly after I moved into my house in 2014. I had very little time to write then. But I had a garage where I kept my bike, so I no longer had to carry it up and down stairs. And I had a new sense of security, a feeling of solidity. I wasn't particularly liquid, but I didn't have to worry about my mortgage as long as I kept my job. I was highly aware, in those first years, of my comfort. And I was uncomfortable with that comfort. I knew from past experience that the discomfort would fade and that my extraordinary new life would become ordinary with time. To stave off that loss, I kept a diary in which I recorded moments of discomfort from my life, usually moments in which I was also enjoying some sort of comfort or pleasure. I wanted to hold on to the discomfort and I wanted to hold on to the comfort, too. This book is what came of that contradiction.

At first, every moment I recorded was excruciating to me, but it was also beautiful. I was sure that my discomfort had something to teach me, and that I would lose some essential knowledge if I let go of the discomfort. I wanted to "stay with the trouble." But I knew that my trouble didn't look like trouble. It looked like what is commonly called "success." This success was the result of having played a particular game, with all the advantages my position afforded. So I regarded my own success and accomplishment with new suspicion.

As I wrote, every word I touched seemed to crumble. I no longer knew what *good* meant, or *art* or *work* or *investment* or *ownership* or *capitalism*. At some point early in my work on this book, my son asked me what *luxury* meant. I told him that it was something you didn't need. No, not like garbage. Something you wanted, that was very nice, but that wasn't necessary to your life. I looked around the room at my house-plants and books. These weren't necessities, but they didn't seem like good examples of luxuries either. The piano was a luxury, but I didn't want to suggest that music wasn't a necessity. "It's like dessert," I told him. "You don't need dessert to live, but it's nice to have. It's a luxury."

Really, the question was a luxury. As was my inability to answer it. "In the affluent society," John Kenneth Galbraith writes, "no useful distinction can be made between luxuries and necessities." All the small necessities of my life, my reading and my writing, were luxuries. And every moment I wrote about was a luxury, though the writing itself felt necessary. I could make no useful distinction between a necessity and a luxury, so I struggled with the word. Later, I looked it up: "The state of great comfort and extravagant living." Maybe I found it difficult to define luxury because I lived in a state of great comfort. This is the state that some people refer to as middle class. And a common euphemism for being upper-middle class or rich is *comfortable*.

Comfortable as I was in my new house, rich as I felt, I didn't have time to write. Not at first. I bargained for time, I made trade-offs for time, and I eventually sold this book to buy time. "I think writers are often terrifying to normal people—that is, to nonwriters in a capitalist system—for this reason: there is almost nothing they will not sell in order to have the time to write," Alexander Chee observes. "Time is our mink, our Lexus, our mansion."

A few names have been changed in this book, in some cases
for technical reasons—to avoid confusion between two friends
named Molly, I modified the spelling of one name to Mollie—
and some names have been avoided or omitted. But for the
most part I chose to use the real first names of my real friends,
many of whom are also writers. This choice was informed in
part by the work of David Trinidad, particularly his book
Notes on a Past Life. Like that book, *Having and Being Had*
was written from a vantage point twenty years removed from
life as a poet in New York City, but where Trinidad is reckoning with his past I'm reckoning with my present.

Many of the names in *Notes on a Past Life* are the names of
poets who, like Trinidad, are associated with the New York
School. An abundance of proper names can be found in the
work of the New York School poet Frank O'Hara, who peo-
pled his poems with artists and writers and friends. A poem
is something that happens between people, O'Hara insisted
in his manifesto for Personism, the movement that he and
Amiri Baraka came up with over lunch. "What was good for
me was that it meant that you could say exactly what was on
your mind and you could say it in a kind of conversational
tone rather than some haughty public tone for public consumption," Baraka said of Personism. For both Baraka and
O'Hara, the tone and texture of intimate conversation was an
aesthetic of resistance.

The tendency of New York School poets to write for and
about one another can be understood as a way of reimagining

importance, of reconfiguring audience, and of refusing conventional notions of what makes poetry "universal." The names that appear in their work recognize a distinct community, which was also, for many of the queer poets of the New York School, an extended family.

Some sense of what it was to belong to such a family is captured in Trinidad's "10 Cherished Books" on the Poetry Foundation blog, where he writes of close encounters with Alice Notley, Ted Berrigan, Dennis Cooper, Allen Ginsberg, James Schuyler, Anne Sexton, Ann Stanford, May Swenson, John Wieners, and Joe Brainard. In the introduction to Trinidad's *Coteries and Gossip*, Jennifer Moxley writes, "Brainard stopped making art in the 1980s because by that time the acts of 'devoted camaraderie' he identified as central to his practice had been replaced by 'quixotic markets of finance, real estate, fashion, and fame.'" For both Trinidad and Brainard, devoted camaraderie between poets is what feeds art, while careerism and capitalism are what starves it.

ON THE RULES:
The metaphor of a game has been used to describe three different kinds of power struggles within capitalism, writes Erik Olin Wright. These are struggles over what game should be played (systemic power), the rules of a given game (institutional power), and moves within a fixed set of rules (situational power). As much as *Having and Being Had* is a record of moves made within a fixed set of rules, it is also a record of my discomfort with those rules and with the game itself. My work

on this book was driven in part by the question of whether it was possible, given the game, to play by my own rules.

As I wrote this book, I established a set of rules for my writing. One of the first rules was that I had to name specific sums whenever I talked about money. Another rule was that I had to talk about money. These rules were a direct refusal of what I understood to be the rules of polite conversation around money: 1) Don't talk about it. 2) If you do talk about it, don't be specific. 3) Minimize what you have. 4) Emphasize that you've earned it. 5) Never forget that work is the story we tell ourselves about money.

Alternative rules of my own invention dictated not just the content of my writing, but also the form and style. Every piece had to begin in the present tense, with a moment drawn from my life. (I allowed myself to break this rule occasionally, particularly when I wanted to write about a book.) And every piece had to include an exchange with another person. Rules also shaped my research. Initially, I allowed myself to read only articles and books given to me or suggested by friends, but as I revised the book I expanded my sources in response to the demands of the work and the questions it raised. Briefly restricting my reading focused my awareness on how my friends extend and limit what I know. My cultural capital is bound up in my social capital—I could not know what I know without who I know, while I would not know who I know without what I know—and both are tied to economic capital. Many of my friends have been educated, as I have, in the values and assumptions and blindnesses of the middle class.

ON THE MIDDLE CLASS:

The term *middle class* is used so widely, and so roughly, that its precise meaning is usually unclear—it might refer to a lifestyle, a value system, a mindset, or an economic bracket. Where exactly that bracket begins and ends is difficult to determine. Economists, sociologists, and the federal government all have different ways of calculating the middle class. In 2018, the US Census Bureau designated as middle class households with incomes between $45,000 and $139,000. Close to half the population fell within that range. Barack Obama's 2012 definition of the middle class included any household making less than $250,000. Congress later expanded that to any household making less than $450,000, which excluded only the top 1 percent of earners from the middle class.

Meanwhile, 40 percent of Americans would struggle to pay an unexpected expense of $400. Income alone is a crude indicator of class, as it doesn't reflect debt or the cost of living or inherited money. Accumulated wealth, or net worth, might serve as a better indicator. The poorest households in this country have a negative net worth, meaning that their debts exceed their assets. According to Edward Wolff, the middle class is composed of households with a net worth between $0 and $471,600. Having experienced both ends of that range, I know as well as anyone that the most significant difference between a net worth of $0 and a net worth of $471,600 is a sense of security.

ON THE WHITES:

My pursuit of the meaning of capitalism in this book was motivated in part by the whiteness of the whale. Ever since the term *white people* was first used in the late seventeenth century in the colonies that would become the United States, that distinction has served to exclude other people from security, ownership, and profit from their own work. Where indentured servants from England and Africa once worked side by side and earned their freedom in this country with their work, the legal category "white people" allowed some servants to continue to earn their freedom while others were denied that freedom.

Without overlooking the significant contribution that non-white interlocutors, artists, and thinkers made to this book, I want to acknowledge that the book is full of white people and their ephemera. I work my way through white artifacts from Greek antiquities to Shaker furniture to the *Titanic* to Scooby-Doo to Dire Straits, and I struggle to wash a white comforter that won't quite come clean. These white materials are the product of a white investigation, meaning not only that the investigator herself is white, but that the prime suspect is a certain kind of white life. There are limits to such an investigation, just as there are limits to what can be learned about the middle class from within the middle class. Even so, my evidence suggests that the stories we tell ourselves about money are full of white lies—not harmless, but white.

ON THE WOMEN:

Emily Dickinson appeared early in my work on this book. I hadn't read her for many years, since I was in college. And then Virginia Woolf showed up, another writer from college. And Gertrude Stein and Alice B. Toklas. And Joan Didion. But Pablo Neruda didn't show up, or Federico García Lorca or Martín Espada or Jack Agüeros, among other writers I had studied. James Joyce made a brief appearance and so did William Faulkner, but the women kept coming back. The women, all modernists, all white and middle class or upper class, seemed to be stand-ins for me. They seemed to allow me to think about aspects of my life and work that would be difficult to think about more directly. These women had once been my models and now were also my cautionary tales. This was particularly true of Virginia Woolf, an essential guide for me as a young writer. The first financial advice I ever received from another woman writer came from Woolf, and I followed it as closely as I could, striving to make £500 a year. I didn't pause to reconsider her advice until I had that income and a room of my own.

ON THE THINGS:

"Next I think that you may object that in all this I have made too much of the importance of material things," Virginia Woolf wrote in *A Room of One's Own*. "Even allowing a generous margin for symbolism, that five hundred a year stands for the power to contemplate, that a lock on the door means the power to think for oneself, still you may say that the mind should rise above such things." The money and the lock and the room were symbolic, but they were also literal. Women writers needed real income, real privacy, and real space for their work. The room of *A Room of One's Own* is what might be called a *literal symbol* in the terminology of poetry. A literal symbol allows for layers of meaning, as it stands for what it is and for something else, too.

The term *true abstraction*, Maggie Nelson writes, could refer to something that is truly abstract, or to something that is abstract in some way and also real or literal or "true." It is with that second sense of the true abstraction that I'm working here, in writing about my life and my things and the concrete abstraction of money, from within my experience of the abstract category "woman," which feels about as real as money. Whether or not that category is real or true has long been a subject of debate among feminists, Nelson notes. I'm grateful for her work, which keeps all the possibilities in play.

ON THE GENRE:

I wondered, as I was writing this book, what it was I was writing. Was it a collection of poems? An essay in episodes? A series of jokes, made at my own expense? A high-stakes game? A midlife crisis? An internal audit? Was it, like Cyril Connolly's book *The Unquiet Grave*, "an experiment in self-dismantling"? Or was it an experiment in refusing the givens of the middle class?

WORKS

ISN'T IT GOOD? (pages 3–6)

"P. S. I Love You," Gordon Jenkins, Johnny Mercer. *Recital by Billie Holiday*, Billie Holiday. Verve Records, 1994.

The Gift: Creativity and the Artist in the Modern World, Lewis Hyde. Vintage, 2007. First published 1983.

"Norwegian Wood (This Bird Has Flown)," John Lennon, Paul McCartney. *Rubber Soul*, The Beatles. Parlophone, 1965.

SLUMMING (pages 7–9)

Mrs. Woolf and the Servants: An Intimate History of Domestic Life in Bloomsbury, Alison Light. Bloomsbury, 2008.
    This extraordinary work informed my writing and thinking throughout *Having and Being Had*. I'm indebted to Light for her insights about the nature of service as well as for her research into Virginia Woolf's servants, life, and time.

THE RIGHT WHITE (pages 15–18)

Color(ed) Theory Suite, Amanda Williams. 2014–2016.

"Art Talk with Visual Artist and Architect Amanda Williams," Paulette Beete. *Art Works Blog*, National Endowment for the Arts. February 17, 2016.

NOT CONSUMERS (pages 19–22)

"Minimalist Art and Articles of Faith," Wendy Moonan. *New York Times*, August 26, 2005.

"Simple Gifts," Joseph Brackett. 1848.

"House Perfect: Is the IKEA Ethos Comfy or Creepy?," Lauren Collins. *The New Yorker*, October 3, 2011.

LIVING THINGS (pages 23–25)

My Life with Things: The Consumer Diaries, Elizabeth Chin. Duke University Press, 2016.

In All My Wildest Dreams, Kemang Wa Lehulere. Art Institute of Chicago, October 27, 2016–January 15, 2017.

CONSUMERS (pages 26–27)

"Consumption," David Graeber. *Current Anthropology*, August 2011.

> All of the information and many of the insights in "Consumers" were drawn from this work, which interrogates the concept of consumption. Graeber asks, "Why is it that when we see someone buying refrigerator magnets and someone else putting on eyeliner or cooking dinner or singing at a karaoke bar or just sitting around watching television, we assume that they are on some level doing the same thing, that it can be

described as 'consumption' or 'consumer behavior,' and that these are all in some way analogous to eating food?"

THANKSGIVING (pages 34–36)

The Gift: Creativity and the Artist in the Modern World, Lewis Hyde. Vintage, 2007. First published 1983.

Hyde notes that Marcel Mauss translated the verb *potlatch* as "to consume."

"Consumption," David Graeber. *Current Anthropology*, August 2011.

About the potlatch, Graeber writes, "Clearly, the spectacle of chiefs vying for titles by setting fire to piles of blankets or other valuables strikes our imagination not so much because it reveals some fundamental truth about human nature largely suppressed in our own society as because it reflects a barely hidden truth about the nature of our own consumer society: that it is largely organized around the ceremonial destruction of commodities." Destruction, Graeber argues, is the legacy of property, the fallout from a long process by which things that were always shared, like land, were legally redefined as things that could be owned. "The ultimate proof of possession, of one's personal *dominium* over a thing," Graeber notes, "is one's ability to destroy it—and indeed this remains one of the key legal ways of defining *dominium*, as a property right, to this day."

"'It Is a Strict Law That Bids Us Dance': Cosmologies, Colonialism, Death, and Ritual Authority in the Kwakwaka'wakw Potlatch, 1849 to 1922," Joseph Masco. *Comparative Studies in Society and History*, 1995.

CAPITALISM (pages 37–40)

The Mushroom at the End of the World: On the Possibility of Life in Capitalist Ruins, Anna Lowenhaupt Tsing. Princeton University Press, 2017.

AFFLUENCE (pages 43–44)

The Affluent Society, John Kenneth Galbraith. Mariner Books, 1998. First published 1958.

Galbraith is responsible for coining the term *conventional wisdom*, which is now in common use. Conventional wisdom is more closely related to convention, in Galbraith's original definition, than it is to wisdom. Conventional wisdom is broadly acceptable, conveniently predictable, and reliably unoriginal. Galbraith spends an entire chapter describing conventional wisdom and then goes on to challenge the conventional wisdom of economics in his time. What I find surprising, in this book from 1958, is that the conventional wisdom of that time sounds very much like the conventional wisdom of our time: Capital must always be allowed to move freely, the production of material goods is of paramount importance, investment in private production should be privileged over investment in public services, the economy must continuously expand, and the degradation of human lives and the natural world is the inevitable cost of that expansion. I would like to believe that some of these notions are proving, with time, to be more destructive than convenient. "The enemy of the conventional wisdom is not ideas," Galbraith writes, "but the march of events."

MORAL MONDAY (pages 45–47)

"Higher Social Class Predicts Increased Unethical Behavior," Paul K. Piff, Daniel M. Stancato, Stéphane Côté, Rodolfo Mendoza-Denton, Dacher Keltner. *Proceedings of the National Academy of Sciences*, March 13, 2012.

"What the Rich Won't Tell You," Rachel Sherman. *New York Times*, September 8, 2017.

THE LANDLORD'S GAME (pages 48–51)

"The Secret History of Monopoly: The Capitalist Board Game's Leftwing Origins," Mary Pilon. *The Guardian*, April 11, 2015.

"For Sale—One Toil-Tired Girl: Highest Bidder Gets Elizabeth Magie." *Boston Daily Globe*, October 11, 1906.

"Girl Who Offers Herself for Sale Gets $100,000 Bid." *St. Louis Post-Dispatch*, October 13, 1906.

"White Slave Would Sell Merely Her Mental Self." *Washington Times*, October 13, 1906.

Progress and Poverty: An Inquiry Into the Cause of Industrial Depressions and of Increase of Want with Increase of Wealth: The Remedy, Henry George. Doubleday & McClure, 1898. First published 1879.

"Board to Page to Board: Native American Antecedents of Two Proprietary Board Games," Philip M. Winkelman. *Board Games Study Journal*, 2016.

The Monopolists: Obsession, Fury, and the Scandal Behind the World's Favorite Board Game, Mary Pilon. Bloomsbury, 2015.

CAPITALISM (pages 52–54)

Capital: A Critique of Political Economy, volume 1, Karl Marx, translated by Ben Fowkes. Penguin Classics, 1992. First published in English in 1867.

Capital in the Twenty-First Century, Thomas Piketty. Belknap Press of Harvard University Press, 2017. First published in English in 2014.

"Economists Clash on Theory, but Will Still Share the Nobel," Binyamin Appelbaum. *New York Times*, October 14, 2013.

"Blame Economists for the Mess We're In," Binyamin Appelbaum. *New York Times*, August 24, 2019.

THE PIANO (pages 57–59)

Men, Women, & Pianos: A Social History, Arthur Loesser. Simon & Schuster, 1954.

WORK (pages 62–65)

"Money for Nothing," Mark Knopfler, Sting. *Brothers in Arms*, Dire Straits. Warner Bros., 1985.

Televised interview, Mark Knopfler. *Parkinson*. BBC1, September 22, 2000.

"Mark Knopfler: Fearless Leader," Ken Tucker, David Fricke. *Rolling Stone*, November 21, 1985.

"Dire Straits' Homophobic Faux-Pas," Sady Doyle. *The Guardian*, January 18, 2011.
    Doyle notes that in one edited version of "Money for Nothing" the word *faggot* is replaced with *mother*.

"Money for Nothing," music video directed by Steve Barron. Pho-nogram Records, 1985.

"In the Gallery," Mark Knopfler. *Dire Straits*, Dire Straits. Warner Bros., 1978.

"'Money for Nothing' Is Not Really Insulting to Homosexuals, Unless They Are Unlucky Enough to Be Working-Class Homo-sexuals," Tom Scocca. *Slate*, January 14, 2011.

Scocca breaks it down beautifully: "The song was marketed with an MTV video in which computer-animated characters disparaged MTV videos—expressing what had previously been Knopfler's actual point of view—which won Video of the Year and helped make the song No. 1. . . . If you're looking for some moment when art and commerce, integrity and 'selling out,' class solidarity and class envy, performer and spectator, content and advertisement, and assorted other tensions all collapsed into a lucrative and critic-proof singularity, you could do worse."

ANYTHING (pages 66–71)

Understanding Class, Erik Olin Wright. Verso, 2015.

Much of "Anything" was drawn from Wright's work, which offers a survey of how sociologists approach class. Wright de-scribes three major approaches: "The first identifies class with the attributes and material conditions of the lives of individu-als. The second focuses on the ways in which social positions give some people control over economic resources of various sorts while excluding others from access to those resources. And the third identifies class, above all, with the ways in which economic positions give some people control over the lives and activities of others."

"A New Model of Social Class? Findings from the BBC's Great British Class Survey Experiment," Mike Savage, Fiona Devine, Niall Cunningham, Mark Taylor, Yaojun Li, Johs. Hjellbrekke, Brigitte Le Roux, Sam Friedman, Andrew Miles. *Sociology*, April 2, 2013.

> This survey uses the term *precariat* to describe the lowest class, the class with the least of three kinds of capital. In his 2011 book *The Precariat*, Guy Standing uses the term to describe a class defined by a lack of security, not a lack of capital. "The precariat is not the bottom of society," he argues. His precariat is a class that cuts across economic classes as they are typically understood. "That somebody has more income than somebody else is not a way to define class," he writes, "nor is lifestyle or access to so-called social capital." Class, for Standing, is defined by security.

"Class Calculator: A US View of the Class System," Michael Goldfarb. *BBC News Magazine*, April 5, 2013.

"Harder for Americans to Rise from Lower Rungs," Jason DeParle. *New York Times*, January 5, 2012.

"Extensive Data Shows Punishing Reach of Racism for Black Boys," Emily Badger, Claire Cain Miller, Adam Pearce, Kevin Quealy. *New York Times*, March 19, 2018.

"Income Mobility Charts for Girls, Asian-Americans and Other Groups. Or Make Your Own," Emily Badger, Claire Cain Miller, Adam Pearce, Kevin Quealy. *New York Times*, March 27, 2018.

PASSING (pages 72–75)

Sapiens: A Brief History of Humankind, Yuval Noah Harari. Harper, 2015.

"The Inescapable Weight of My $100,000 Student Debt," M. H. Miller. *The Guardian*, August 21, 2018.

My Life with Things: The Consumer Diaries, Elizabeth Chin. Duke University Press, 2016.

> Throughout *Having and Being Had*, most of my information about Marx is drawn from Chin's research into Marx's domestic life and consumption. Chin is particularly interested in Marx's contradictions, as they help her think about her own contradictions. I, in turn, am interested in both Chin's contradictions and Marx's contradictions.

MEMBERSHIP (pages 76–77)

Venus de Milo with Drawers, Salvador Dalí. 1936.

RICH (pages 81–83)

"Here's How Much Money You Have to Earn to be Considered Rich in 42 Major US Cities," Abby Jackson, Dominic-Madori Davis. *Business Insider*, December 9, 2019.

My Life with Things: The Consumer Diaries, Elizabeth Chin. Duke University Press, 2016.

"A Promise Unfulfilled at an Art Deco Bathhouse in the Rockaways," Lisa W. Foderaro. *New York Times*, August 21, 2012.

Käthe Kollwitz, *Woman with Dead Child*. 1903.

LEISURE (pages 87–89)

"Aristotle on *Schole* and *Nous* as a Way of Life," Kostas Kalimtzis. *Organon*, 2013.

On leisure, Kalimtzis writes, "Leisure is not preparation but an end *possessed*, and in fact the very word *scholê*, according to some scholars, may be derived from the verb *echein* which means *to have* or *to possess*."

Politics, Aristotle, translated by Benjamin Jowett. Digireads.com Publishing, 2017.

The Theory of the Leisure Class, Thorstein Veblen. Oxford University Press, 2007. First published 1899.

The Affluent Society, John Kenneth Galbraith. Mariner Books, 1998. First published 1958.

THE PROTESTANT ETHIC (pages 90–91)

The Protestant Ethic and the Spirit of Capitalism, Max Weber, translated by Stephen Kalberg. Oxford University Press, 2010. First published 1905.

"Why Work?," Elizabeth Kolbert. *The New Yorker*, November 22, 2004.

WORK (pages 92–93)

"Bartleby the Scrivener: A Story of Wall-Street," Herman Melville. *The Piazza Tales*. Dix & Edwards, 1856.

David, Michelangelo. 1501–1504.

Augustus of Prima Porta, unknown artist. First century AD.

The Thinker, Auguste Rodin. 1903.

CAPITALISM (pages 94–95)

A History of the World in Seven Cheap Things: A Guide to Capitalism, Nature, and the Future of the Planet, Raj Patel, Jason W. Moore. University of California Press, 2017.

"The New Abolitionism," Chris Hayes. *The Nation*, April 22, 2014.

LIBERATION COLLECTION (pages 96–98)

They Were Her Property: White Women as Slave Owners in the American South, Stephanie E. Jones-Rogers. Yale University Press, 2019.

"Resistance of the Object: Aunt Hester's Scream," Fred Moten. *In the Break: The Aesthetics of the Black Radical Tradition*. University of Minnesota Press, 2003.

"For One Springfield Woman, a Complicated Desire to Preserve Racist Emblems," Ben James. *WBUR News*, January 15, 2018.

"Shocker: DNA Test Proves Mrs. Butterworth Isn't Black," Bill Matthews. *The Peoples News*, February 24, 2010.

WORK (pages 99–101)

The Gift: Creativity and the Artist in the Modern World, Lewis Hyde. Vintage, 2007. First published 1983.

Work: The Last 1,000 Years, Andrea Komlosy. Verso, 2018.

Capital: A Critique of Political Economy, volume 1, Karl Marx, translated by Ben Fowkes. Penguin Classics, 1992. First published in English in 1867.

DRAG (pages 102–105)

Paris Is Burning, directed by Jennie Livingston. Off White Productions, 1990.

"Supermodel (You Better Work)," RuPaul, Jimmy Harry, Larry Tee. *Supermodel of the World,* RuPaul. Tommy Boy Records, 1992.

"Supermodel (You Better Work)," music video directed by Randy Barbato. Tommy Boy Records, 1993.

"RuPaul: The King of Queens," Mac McClelland. *Rolling Stone,* October 4, 2013.

"Is 'RuPaul's Drag Race' the Most Radical Show on TV?," Jenna Wortham. *New York Times Magazine,* January 24, 2018.

"RuPaul: 'Drag Is a Big F-You to Male-Dominated Culture,'" Decca Aitkenhead. *The Guardian,* March 3, 2018.

"Work," Jahron Brathwaite, Matthew Samuels, Allen Ritter, Rupert Thomas, Jr., Aubrey Graham, Robyn Fenty, Monte Moir. *Anti,* Rihanna. Roc Nation, 2016.

"How Rihanna's 'Work' Works," Spencer Kornhaber. *The Atlantic,* January 27, 2016.

"Work," music video directed by Director X. Roc Nation, 2016.

"Work," music video directed by Tim Erem. Roc Nation, 2016.

THE WITCH (pages 106–109)

Mother Russia: The Feminine Myth in Russian Culture, Joanna Hubbs. Indiana University Press, 1988.

Caliban and the Witch: Women, the Body and Primitive Accumulation, Silvia Federici. Autonomedia, 2014. First published 2004.

> Most of the historical information in "The Witch" was drawn from Federici's remarkable history of women during the transition from feudalism to capitalism. She writes, "Female serfs were less dependent on their male kin, less differentiated from them physically, socially, and psychologically, and were less subservient to men's needs than 'free' women were to be later in capitalist society."

Witches, Witch-Hunting, and Women, Silvia Federici. PM Press, 2018.

MOTHER'S HELPER (pages 110–113)

Mrs. Woolf and the Servants, Alison Light. Bloomsbury, 2008.

End Slavery Now, www.endslaverynow.org.

JOAN DIDION (pages 114–116)

"The Autumn of Joan Didion," Caitlin Flanagan. *The Atlantic*, January/February 2012.

"The White Album," Joan Didion. *The White Album*. Farrar, Straus and Giroux, 1990. First published 1979.

"Slouching Towards Bethlehem," Joan Didion. *Slouching Towards Bethlehem*. Farrar, Straus and Giroux, 1990. First published 1961.

"Out of Bethlehem: The Radicalization of Joan Didion," Louis Menand. *The New Yorker*, August 17, 2015.

Menand notes, "Most of the people who walked around the
Village looking like Beats in 1960, like most of the people who
walked around San Francisco or Berkeley or Cambridge looking like hippies in 1967, were weekend dropouts. They were
contingent rebels. They put on the costumes; they went to the
concerts and got high; and then they went back to school or
back to work. It was a life style, not a life."

"New York: Sentimental Journeys," Joan Didion. *New York Review
of Books*, January 17, 1991.

TEA (pages 117–119)

Lauren Kalman: But if the Crime Is Beautiful . . . , Lauren Kalman.
Museum of Arts and Design, New York, October 20, 2016–March
15, 2017.

Stone Deaf, Milena Bonilla. *The Arcades: Contemporary Art and
Walter Benjamin*. Jewish Museum, New York, March 17–August
6, 2017.

Sweetness and Power: The Place of Sugar in Modern History, Sidney
W. Mintz. Penguin Books, 1986.
    All the historical information about tea and tea consumption
    in "Tea" is drawn from this extraordinary work.

I'm Nobody! Who Are You? The Life and Poetry of Emily Dickinson.
Morgan Library & Museum, New York, January 20–May 28, 2017.

My Wars Are Laid Away in Books: The Life of Emily Dickinson,
Alfred Habegger. Modern Library, 2002.
    Habegger notes that Dickinson had opportunities to pub-
    lish and chose not to. He speculates on a number of reasons

for this, including the conventions of the time. "It is not the case that Dickinson was denied an outlet, or that her work was deemed too 'modern' or 'incorrect' or 'daring' to be published in her time. As Karen Dandurand and Joanne Dobson have shown, many conservative nineteenth-century Americans continued to hold the old idea that the best sort of writing circulates in private."

"I'm Nobody! Who are you?" (260), Emily Dickinson. *The Poems of Emily Dickinson: Reading Edition*, edited by R. W. Franklin. Belknap Press of Harvard University Press, 1999.

Critical Companion to Emily Dickinson: A Literary Reference to Her Life and Work, Sharon Leiter. Facts on File, 2006.

MINE (pages 120–122)

"I am afraid to own a Body" (1050), Emily Dickinson. *The Poems of Emily Dickinson: Reading Edition*, edited by R. W. Franklin. Belknap Press of Harvard University Press, 1999.

"The World Is Too Much with Us," William Wordsworth. *Poems, in Two Volumes*. Longman, Hurst, Rees, and Orme, 1807.

"The Bean Eaters," Gwendolyn Brooks. *Selected Poems*. Harper & Row, 1963.

"The Emperor of Ice Cream," Wallace Stevens. *The Collected Poems of Wallace Stevens*. Knopf, 1982.

"Mine—by the Right of the White Election" (411), Emily Dickinson. *The Poems of Emily Dickinson: Reading Edition*, edited by R. W. Franklin. Belknap Press of Harvard University Press, 1999.

Emily Dickinson: Personae and Performance, Elizabeth Phillips. Penn State University Press, 1988.

"I had some things that I called mine" (101), Emily Dickinson. *The Poems of Emily Dickinson: Reading Edition*, edited by R. W. Franklin. Belknap Press of Harvard University Press, 1999.
> The index to the first lines of Dickinson's poems at the back of this work reads in part: ". . . I had a daily bliss / I had a guinea golden / I had been hungry all the years / I had no cause to be awake / I had no time to hate / I had not minded walls / I had some things that I called mine . . ."

"'Some Things That I Called Mine': Dickinson and the Perils of Property Ownership," James R. Guthrie, *The Emily Dickinson Journal*, Fall 2000.

MASTERED (pages 128–130)

The Gift: Creativity and the Artist in the Modern World, Lewis Hyde. Vintage, 2007. First published 1983.

"On the Origins of the Northern European Notion of Paid Labor as Necessary to the Full Formation of an Adult Human Being," David Graeber. *Bullshit Jobs: A Theory*. Simon & Schuster, 2018.

Mrs. Woolf and the Servants, Alison Light. Bloomsbury, 2008.
> Light writes, "When I first had the idea for this book a dozen or so years ago, I found it hard to think of domestic service except as exploitation, a species of psychological and emotional slavery—'dependency,' with its pejorative overtones, would be a more appropriate term." But then her husband fell ill and she cared for him through the end of his life, in the process coming to think that not all service is about oppression. "Dependence

was no longer a question of whether, so much as when. And I also came to think that the capacity to entrust one's life to the care of others, including strangers, and for this to happen safely and in comfort, without abuse, is crucial to any decent community and to any society worth its name."

WORK (pages 131–134)

"A Composer and His Wife: Creativity through Kink," Zachary Woolfe. *New York Times*, February 24, 2016.

My Life with Things: The Consumer Diaries, Elizabeth Chin. Duke University Press, 2016.

Love and Capital, Mary Gabriel. Little, Brown and Company, 2011.

"Manifesto for Maintenance Art 1969!," Mierle Laderman Ukeles. 1969.

SERVICE (pages 135–138)

"A Composer and His Wife: Creativity through Kink," Zachary Woolfe. *New York Times*, February 24, 2016.

"'Race Play': Hitting the Mainstream Media . . . ?," Mollena Williams-Haas. *The Perverted Negress*, April 11, 2013.

"Playground 2015 Closing Keynote," Mollena Williams-Haas, Georg Friederich Haas. YouTube, November 19, 2015.

"Master/slave Relationships and Taboo BDSM Play: A Conversation with Mollena Williams-Haas," Evie Lupine, Mollena Williams-Haas. Kinkfest interview series. YouTube, April 10, 2019.

"When Prejudice Is Sexy: Inside the Kinky World of Race-Play," Anna North. *Jezebel*, March 14, 2012.

"Nothing to Earn," Mollena Williams-Haas. *The Perverted Negress*, November 5, 2016.

SATISFACTION (pages 139–143)

The Alice B. Toklas Cook Book, Alice B. Toklas. Harper Perennial, 1984. First published 1954.

Two Lives: Gertrude and Alice, Janet Malcolm. Yale University Press, 2007.

"Strangers in Paradise," Janet Malcolm. *The New Yorker*, November 6, 2006.

TOIL (pages 144–146)

The Affluent Society, John Kenneth Galbraith. Mariner Books, 1998. First published 1958.

"Undocumented, Vulnerable, Scared: The Women Who Pick Your Food for \$3 an Hour," Shannon Sims, Verónica G. Cárdenas-Vento. *The Guardian*, July 10, 2019.

WORK (pages 147–151)

The Affluent Society, John Kenneth Galbraith. Mariner Books, 1998. First published 1958.

Working: People Talk About What They Do All Day and How They Feel About What They Do, Studs Terkel. Pantheon Books, 1974.

Bullshit Jobs: A Theory, David Graeber. Simon & Schuster, 2018.

Graeber notes, "In the year 1930, John Maynard Keynes predicted that, by century's end, technology would have advanced sufficiently that countries like Great Britain or the United States would have achieved a fifteen-hour work week. There's every reason to believe he was right. In technological terms, we are quite capable of this."

"Crafting a Job: Revisioning Employees as Active Crafters of Their Work," Amy Wrzesniewski, Jane E. Dutton. *Academy of Management Review*, April 2001.

"Being Valued and Devalued at Work: A Social Valuing Perspective," Jane E. Dutton, Gelaye Debebe, Amy Wrzesniewski. *Qualitative Organizational Research, Volume 3: Best Papers from the Davis Conference on Qualitative Research*, edited by Beth A. Bechky, Kimberly D. Elsbach. IAP, 2016.

"What's the Most Satisfying Job in the World? You'd Be Surprised," Barry Schwartz. ideas.ted.com, September 8, 2015.

PLAY (pages 152–154)

"Explore the Neighborhood of Make-Believe," www.misterrogers.org.

"Children's Risky Play from an Evolutionary Perspective: The Anti-Phobic Effects of Thrilling Experiences," Ellen Beate Hansen Sandseter, Leif Edward Ottesen Kennair. *Evolutionary Psychology*, April 1, 2011.

ART (pages 155–157)

"Two Tramps in Mud Time," Robert Frost. *The Complete Poems of Robert Frost*. Henry Holt & Co., 1949.

WORK (pages 163–164)

The Theory of the Leisure Class, Thorstein Veblen. Oxford University Press, 2007. First published 1899.

1493: Uncovering the New World Columbus Created, Charles C. Mann. Vintage, 2012.

BARTLEBY (pages 165–167)

"Bartleby the Scrivener: A Story of Wall-Street," Herman Melville. *The Piazza Tales*. Dix & Edwards, 1856.

"Preferring Not To: The Paradox of Passive Resistance in Herman Melville's 'Bartleby,'" Jane Desmarais. *Journal of the Short Story in English*, Spring 2001.

INVESTMENT (pages 168–169)

Dracula, screenplay by Garrett Fort, directed by Tod Browning. Universal Pictures, 1931.

Dracula, Bram Stoker. Dover, 2000. First published 1897.

WELCOME TO THE JUNGLE (pages 170–173)

"No," Meghan Trainor, Eric Frederic, Jacob Kasher. *Thank You*, Meghan Trainor. Epic, 2016.

"Biography," Frances Willard House Museum, Chicago, https://franceswillardhouse.org.

"'Lesbian-Like' and the Social History of Lesbianisms," Judith M. Bennett. *Journal of the History of Sexuality*, January 2000.

I borrowed Bennett's use of the term *lesbian-like* to describe Frances Willard. In thinking about queer lives from other eras, she writes, "I suggest that we try broadening our perspective to include women whom I have chosen to call 'lesbian-like': women whose lives might have particularly offered opportunities for same-sex love; women who resisted norms of feminine behavior based on heterosexual marriage; women who lived in circumstances that allowed them to nurture and support other women."

"Truth Telling: Frances Willard and Ida B. Wells," Frances Willard House Museum, Chicago, https://franceswillardhouse.org.

"Ida B. Wells and the Lynching of Black Women," Crystal N. Feimster. *New York Times*, April 28, 2018.

"You Don't Own Me," John Medora, David White. *Lesley Gore Sings of Mixed-Up Hearts*, Lesley Gore. Mercury, 1963.

"Welcome to the Jungle," Guns N' Roses. *Appetite for Destruction*, Guns N' Roses. Geffen, 1987.

MAINTENANCE (pages 174–177)

Hartford Wash: Washing, Tracks, Maintenance—Outside and Inside, Mierle Laderman Ukeles. 1973.

"Manifesto for Maintenance: A Conversation with Mierle Laderman Ukeles," Bartholomew Ryan. *Art in America*, March 18, 2009.

Touch Sanitation Performance, Mierle Laderman Ukeles. 1979–1980.

"Manifesto for Maintenance Art 1969!," Mierle Laderman Ukeles. 1969.

Visiting Artist Program, Mierle Laderman Ukeles. School of the Art Institute of Chicago, September 24, 2019.

I Make Maintenance Art One Hour Every Day, Mierle Laderman Ukeles. *Art < > World*, Whitney Museum Downtown, New York, September 16–October 20, 1976.

"How Mierle Laderman Ukeles Turned Maintenance Work into Art," Jillian Steinhauer. *Hyperallergic*, February 10, 2017.

SIN STOCKS (pages 178–180)

"When Sears Flourished, So Did Workers. At Amazon, It's More Complicated," Nelson Schwartz, Michael Corkery. *New York Times*, October 23, 2018.

INTEGRITY (pages 181–183)

"The Bell," Eric Dean Wilson. 2019.
> Many of the details in "Integrity" were borrowed from an email written to me by Wilson. He generously allowed me to use this material, which also appears in his work "The Bell," currently pending publication.

"For the Sake of Life on Earth, We Must Put a Limit on Wealth," George Monbiot. *The Guardian*, September 19, 2019.
> Monbiot writes, "A series of research papers shows that income is by far the most important determinant of environmental impact. . . . Though they are disproportionately responsible for our environmental crises, the rich will be hurt least and last by planetary disaster, while the poor are hurt first and worst. The richer people are, the research suggests, the less such knowledge is likely to trouble them."

"Meet the Leftish Economist with a New Story about Capitalism," Katy Lederer. *New York Times*, November 26, 2019.

The Value of Everything: Making and Taking in the Global Economy, Mariana Mazzucato. Penguin Books, 2019.

SPY VS. SPY (pages 184–185)

Spy vs. Spy: The Complete Casebook, Antonio Prohías. Watson-Guptill, 2001.

APOCALYPSE NOW (pages 186–187)

Apocalypse Now, screenplay by John Milius, Francis Ford Coppola, directed by Francis Ford Coppola. Omni Zoetrope, 1979.

GREAT AMERICA (pages 188–189)

"The Water-Park Scandal and Two Americas in the Raw: Are We a Nation of Line-Cutters, or Are We the Line?," Tom Junod. *Esquire*, September 5, 2012.

"Pilot," written by Joe Weisberg, directed by Gavin O'Connor. *The Americans*. Season 1, episode 1. FX, January 30, 2013.

CAPITALISM (pages 190–191)

"A Tiki Scare Is No Fair," Joe Ruby, Ken Spears. *Scooby-Doo, Where Are You!*. Season 2, episode 6. CBS, October 17, 1970.

"Mine Your Own Business," Joe Ruby, Ken Spears. *Scooby-Doo, Where Are You!*. Season 1, episode 4. CBS, October 4, 1969.

WORKS

TITANIC (pages 192–193)

"Unsinkable," Daniel Mendelsohn. *The New Yorker*, April 9, 2012.

REPEAT (pages 194–195)

"The Thrill Is Gone," Rick Darnell, Roy Hawkins. *Completely Well*, B. B. King. Bluesway/ABC Records, 1969.

"I'll Come Running," Brian Eno. *Another Green World*, Brian Eno. Island, 1975.

ART (pages 196–199)

"Midnight Lace #2," Philip Monaghan. "The Late Show" Project, 2010–2015.

"The Late Show," David Trinidad. *The Late Show*. Turtle Point Press, 2007.

"Peyton Place: A Haiku Soap Opera," John Bresland. *Blackbird*, 2015.

Peyton Place: A Haiku Soap Opera, David Trinidad. Turtle Point Press, 2013.

ONE'S OWN (pages 200–202)

A Room of One's Own, Virginia Woolf. Hogarth Press, 1935.

Mrs. Woolf and the Servants, Alison Light. Bloomsbury, 2008.
  Despite not having the freedom to write, despite Woolf's assertion that the lower classes didn't produce literature, a woman Woolf's sister described as "almost incredibly stupid" drafted a novel about working for that sister as a governess.

The half-finished novel was discovered after the governess left, but it was not preserved for history, so we know only that Woolf's sister found it a work of "extraordinary bitterness."

GUGGENHEIM (pages 203–205)

"Peggy Guggenheim Influencer Overview and Analysis," Rebecca Seiferle. *The Art Story*, www.theartstory.org. December 26, 2018.

Peggy Guggenheim: The Shock of the Modern, Francine Prose. Yale University Press, 2015.

CAPITALISM (pages 206–209)

Debt: The First 5,000 Years, David Graeber. Melville House, 2014.

"Were the Jews Moneylenders Out of Necessity?," Maristella Botticini, Zvi Eckstein. *Reform Judaism*, Spring 2013.

Caliban and the Witch: Women, the Body and Primitive Accumulation, Silvia Federici. Autonomedia, 2014. First published 2004.
   On the social status of Jewish people in the twelfth century, Federici writes, "There is, in fact, a revealing correlation between the displacement of the Jews by Christian competitors, as moneylenders to Kings, popes and the higher clergy, and the new discriminatory rules (e.g., the wearing of distinctive clothing) that were adopted against them, as well as their expulsion from England and France. Degraded by the Church, further separated by the Christian population, and forced to confine their moneylending (one of the few occupations available to them) to the village level, the Jews became an easy target for indebted peasants, who often vented on them their anger against the rich."

"The Usurer and the Merchant Prince: Italian Businessmen and the Ecclesiastical Law of Restitution, 1100–1550," Benjamin N. Nelson. *Journal of Economic History*, 1947.

The Gift: Creativity and the Artist in the Modern World, Lewis Hyde. Vintage, 2007. First published 1983.

"How Toni Morrison Fostered a Generation of Black Writers," Hilton Als. *The New Yorker*, October 27, 2003.

ART (pages 213–215)

Debt to Society: Accounting for Life under Capitalism, Miranda Joseph. University of Minnesota Press, 2014.

"Free Flight," June Jordan. *Passion*. Beacon Press, 1980.

EAT A PEACH (pages 216–218)

James and the Giant Peach, screenplay by Karey Kirkpatrick, Jonathan Roberts, Steve Bloom, directed by Henry Selick. Walt Disney Pictures, 1996.

Eat a Peach, The Allman Brothers Band. Capricorn, 1971.

The Unquiet Grave: A Word Cycle, Cyril Connolly (Palinurus, pseudonym). Hamish Hamilton, 1946.

"The Love Song of J. Alfred Prufrock," T. S. Eliot. *Collected Poems 1909–1962*. Harcourt, 1963.

ACCOUNTING (pages 219–222)

"Karl Marx Considers His Prospects" (postcard), *Cabinet*, Summer 2013.

Income's Outcome, Danica Phelps. 2012– (ongoing).

"Income's Outcome," Danica Phelps. www.danicaphelpsprojects .com.

The Cost of Love, Danica Phelps. 2012.

"From Paint to Pixels," Jacoba Urist. *The Atlantic*, May 14, 2015.

"About the Exhibition: Danica Phelps, *Mark Down*, September 12–October 17, 2009," Galerie Judin, Berlin. www.galerie judin.com.

"The Art Market Doesn't Want Us to Ask Where the Money Comes From," Barbara Bourland. *Literary Hub*, July 2, 2019.

"Danica Phelps. Income's Outcome September 19–December 10, 2013," Nieves Fernández, Madrid. www.nfgaleria.com.

CAPITALISM (pages 223–226)

Debt: The First 5,000 Years, David Graeber. Melville House, 2014. Graeber slightly rewords a phrase from Marx, who wrote in his 1875 *Critique of the Gotha Program*: "From each according to his ability, to each according to his needs." This phrase did not originate with Marx—it was a socialist slogan.

The World Turned Upside Down: Radical Ideas During the English Revolution, Christopher Hill. Penguin Books, 1991. First published 1972.

"Which Way to the City on a Hill?," Marilynne Robinson. *New York Review of Books*, July 18, 2019. Robinson observes that the word *Puritan*, like the word *capitalism*, is one of those words that we tend to use without really knowing what it means. *Liberal* is as well, as she notes: "The word 'liberal' and its forms were used in American social thought until quite recently to refer to a scripturally blessed and commanded open-handedness, a generosity based in faith and love. Over time, the word became secularized with use, though it retained its essential meaning. Then someone noticed that when an Englishman used the word it meant something else entirely and was properly, by our lights, a term of opprobrium. And it was banished from use by those alert to the possibility that a gaffe had been made. So our tradition became unreadable in its own terms, capitalist in the light of a new hermeneutics that sees context as special pleading."

Caliban and the Witch: Women, the Body and Primitive Accumulation, Silvia Federici. Autonomedia, 2014. First published 2004.

WHITE RUSSIANS (pages 227–228)

Revoliutsiia! Demonstratsiia! Soviet Art Put to the Test. Art Institute of Chicago, October 29, 2017–January 15, 2018.

I Am Not Your Negro, written by James Baldwin, Raoul Peck, directed by Raoul Peck. Magnolia Pictures, 2016.

Beat the Whites with the Red Wedge, El Lissitzky. 1919.

SPIES (pages 229–233)

"Inheritance," Alexander Chee. *How to Write an Autobiographical Novel: Essays*. Mariner Books, 2018.

The Captive Mind, Czesław Miłosz. Vintage Books, 1955.

"'Ketman' and Doublethink: What It Costs to Comply with Tyranny," Jacob Mikanowski. *Aeon*, October 9, 2017.

Race Diplomacy: African American International Diplomacy, 1855–1955, Athan Biss. Dissertation submitted for the degree of Doctor of Philosophy (History). University of Wisconsin-Madison, 2018.
> All of my information about Homer Smith's life was drawn from this work, which includes original research conducted at the Russian State Archive of Socio-Political History in Moscow.

"Negroes in Russia Devoted to Stalin," Homer Smith (Chatwood Hall, pseudonym). *Pittsburgh Courier*, July 31, 1937.
> Smith's writing was marked by, as Athan Biss puts it, "the stylistic deficiencies that afflict the prose of political propagandists."

"Introduction: The Price of the Ticket," James Baldwin. *The Price of the Ticket: Collected Nonfiction, 1948–1985*. St. Martin's Press, 1985.

CITIZENS (pages 234–236)

The World Falls Away, Wanda Coleman. University of Pittsburgh Press, 2011.

Manifesto of the Communist Party, Karl Marx, Friedrich Engels. *Marx/Engels Selected Works*, volume 1. Progress Publishers, 1969. First published 1848.

The Mushroom at the End of the World: On the Possibility of Life in Capitalist Ruins, Anna Lowenhaupt Tsing. Princeton University Press, 2017.

The Precariat: The New Dangerous Class, Guy Standing. Bloomsbury Academic, 2011.

WATER (pages 237–238)

An Inquiry into the Nature and Causes of the Wealth of Nations, volume 1, Adam Smith. Liberty Fund, 2009. First Published 1776.

ART (pages 239–241)

The Coronation of the Emperor Napoleon I and the Crowning of the Empress Joséphine in Notre-Dame Cathedral on December 2, 1804, Jacques-Louis David. 1807.

"Apeshit," music video directed by Ricky Saiz. Parkwood, Roc Nation, 2018.

"Boss," Beyoncé, Shawn Carter, Tyrone Griffin, Jr., Dernst Emile II. *Everything Is Love*, the Carters. Parkwood, Sony, Roc Nation, 2018.

"Apeshit," Pharrell Williams, Beyoncé, Shawn Carter, Quavious Keyate Marshall, Kiari Kendrell Cephus. *Everything Is Love*, the Carters. Parkwood, Sony, Roc Nation, 2018.

The Raft of the Medusa, Théodore Géricault. 1818–1819.

The Massacre at Chios, Eugène Delacroix. 1824.

Venus de Milo, Alexandros of Antioch. 101 BC.

"Art and Property Now," John Berger. *Landscapes: John Berger on Art*. Verso, 2016.

BLOOD (pages 242–245)

"The Tragedy of the Commons," Garrett Hardin. *Science*, December 13, 1968.

BICYCLE MANIFESTO (pages 246–250)

"Interview with Cauleen Smith and Brandon Breaux," Hans-Ulrich Obrist, Cauleen Smith, Brandon Breaux. *Creative Chicago: An Interview Marathon*, Hans-Ulrich Obrist, Alison Cuddy. Terra Foundation for American Art, 2019.

"What Driving Can Teach Us about Living," Rachel Cusk. *New York Times*, January 3, 2019.

THE HUG (pages 251–253)

This Is Not a Novel, David Markson. Counterpoint, 2001.

Dictée, Theresa Hak Kyung Cha. Tanam Press, 1982.

Pond, Claire-Louise Bennett. Riverhead Books, 2017.

Holy Land: A Suburban Memoir, D. J. Waldie. W. W. Norton & Company, 1996.

Outline: A Novel, Rachel Cusk. Farrar, Straus and Giroux, 2014.

Agaat, Marlene van Niekerk, translated by Michiel Heyns. Tin House Books, 2010.

RESIGNATION (pages 254–256)

"William Faulkner Was Really Bad at Being a Postman," Emily Temple. *Literary Hub*, September 25, 2018.

As I Lay Dying, William Faulkner. Vintage, 1990. First published 1930.

WORK (pages 257–258)

"She Works Hard for the Money," Donna Summer, Michael Omartian. *She Works Hard for the Money*, Donna Summer. Mercury, 1983.

"She Works Hard for the Money," music video directed by Brian Grant. Mercury, 1983.

ALL I WANTED (pages 259–261)

"Emily Dickinson Face to Face: Unpublished Letters with Notes and Reminiscences," Martha Dickinson Bianchi. *Emily Dickinson: Critical Assessments*, volume 2, edited by Graham Clarke. Helm Information, 2002.

"I'm Nobody! Who are you?" (260), Emily Dickinson. *The Poems of Emily Dickinson: Reading Edition*, edited by R. W. Franklin. Belknap Press of Harvard University Press, 1999.

"Repulsed by Pharma-Bro Martin Shkreli? Maybe You Also Hate Capitalism," Jesse Myerson. *In These Times*, February 22, 2016.
> Of Shkreli's purchase of the Wu-Tang album, Myerson writes, "The situation was obviously unique in its particulars, but one essential element of it is highly precedented, even endemic to American 'racial capitalism': cultural appropriation." He defines cultural appropriation as "the transformation of one person's culture into another's *property*."

Peyton Place: A Haiku Soap Opera, David Trinidad. Turtle Point Press, 2013.

WORKS

THE GIFT (pages 266–268)

The Law of Freedom in a Platform; or, True Magistracy Restored, Gerrard Winstanley. 1652.

The Gift: Creativity and the Artist in the Modern World, Lewis Hyde. Vintage, 2007. First published 1983.

CONSUMPTION (pages 269–272)

My Wars Are Laid Away in Books: The Life of Emily Dickinson, Alfred Habegger. Modern Library, 2002.

> The quote from Dickinson that ends "Consumption" is from a draft of a letter to Otis Phillips Lord. The full fragment reads, "Dont you know you are happiest while I withhold and not confer—dont you know that 'No' is the wildest word we consign to Language? / You do, for you know all things." Habegger notes, "Whoever preserved the manuscript containing these important words wanted them and nothing else: the paper has been scissored top and bottom."

"Blame Economists for the Mess We're In," Binyamin Appelbaum. *New York Times*, August 24, 2019.

THE HOLE (pages 273–277)

The Unquiet Grave: A Word Cycle, Cyril Connolly (Palinurus, pseudonym). Hamish Hamilton, 1946.

"At the Dam," Joan Didion. *The White Album*. Farrar, Straus and Giroux, 1990. First published 1979.

NOTES (pages 279–288)

A Woman of Property, Robyn Schiff. Penguin Books, 2016.

The Affluent Society, John Kenneth Galbraith. Mariner Books, 1998. First published 1958.

"Imposter," Alexander Chee. *How to Write an Autobiographical Novel: Essays*. Mariner Books, 2018.

Frank O'Hara: The Poetics of Coterie, Lytle Shaw. University of Iowa Press, 2016.

Coteries and Gossip, David Trinidad. Split Series, volume 4. The Lettered Streets Press, 2019.

Understanding Class, Erik Olin Wright. Verso, 2015.

"What Is Considered Middle Class Income?," Kimberly Amadeo. *The Balance*, June 18, 2019.

"Household Wealth Trends in the United States, 1962–2016: Has Middle Class Wealth Recovered?," Edward Wolff. National Bureau of Economic Research Working Paper No. 24085, November 2017.

A Room of One's Own, Virginia Woolf. Hogarth Press, 1935.

Women, the New York School, and Other True Abstractions, Maggie Nelson. University of Iowa Press, 2011.

PEOPLE

Everyday exchanges with other writers, artists, scholars, and citizen thinkers served as my primary source of information and ideas for this book. I'm indebted to these informants: Hillary Aarons, Athan Biss, Mavis Biss, Roger Biss, Brian Bouldrey, Ethan Boxley, John Bresland, Juneau Bresland, Min Li Chan, Dan Cooper, Nick Davis, Emma Dolan, Leo Ferguson, Jennifer Francis, Chris Gaggero, Bill Girard, Ellen Graf, Daryl Haggard, Molly Hein, Jim Hodge, Michelle Huang, Noel Ignatiev, Ben James, Emir Kamenica, Karla Kelsey, Drew Langsner, Sara Levine, Joshua Mehigan, Nami Mun, Mara Naselli, Maggie Nelson, Vojislav Pejović, Ben Piekut, Susannah Pratt, Robyn Schiff, Shauna Seliy, Lisa Solar, Barry Sorkin, Molly Tambor, David Trinidad, Chris Vatalaro, Connie Voisine, Ivana Vukojicic, Wendy Wall, Will West, Eric Dean Wilson, and Mark Witte.

Mara Naselli read multiple drafts and worked closely with me during the final stages of revision. I'm grateful to her and to the generous readers whose responses shaped this book along the way: Mavis Biss, John Bresland, Suzanne Buffam, Min Li Chan, Stuart Dybek, Amy Leach, Matt McGowan, Nami Mun,

Susannah Pratt, Glen Retief, Robyn Schiff, and David Trinidad. Thanks to Maggie Nelson for a good, tough critique of the first draft. And thanks to Deb Gorlin for over twenty years of encouragement.

Thanks to John Freeman at *Freeman's* for publishing early versions of "Work" and "Service" and to Arda Collins at *Jubilat* for publishing early versions of "Comforter," "Poor," "Titanic," and "Ancient Mew." Thanks to Zoe Johnson for excellent assistance with fact-checking. Thanks to all the staff at Ragdale for giving me a place to work and for feeding me so well. Thanks to Matt McGowan for supporting this project from the very beginning and for seeing me through a crisis in confidence. Thanks to Cal Morgan for patient guidance and for giving me the time I needed to do this work.